Instructional Coaches & Classroom Teachers

Sharing the Road to Success

Authors

Cheryl Jones, M.Ed. and Mary Vreeman, M.A.

Foreword by Ellin Oliver Keene, M.A.

SHELL EDUCATION

Instructional Coaches and Classroom Teachers: Sharing the Road to Success

Editor
Joan Irwin, M.A.

Assistant Editor
Leslie Huber, M.A.

Editorial Director
Lori Kamola, M.S.Ed.

Editor-in-Chief
Sharon Coan, M.S.Ed.

Editorial Manager
Gisela Lee, M.A.

Creative Director
Lee Aucoin

Cover Design
Lee Aucoin

Print Production Manager
Don Tran

Interior Layout Designer
Robin Erickson

Print Production
Juan Chavolla

Publisher
Corinne Burton, M.A.Ed.

Image Credits: All photographs provided by the authors with permission

---

Shell Education
5301 Oceanus Drive
Huntington Beach, CA 92649-1030
http://www.shelleducation.com
ISBN 978-1-4258-0332-2
© *2008 Shell Education*
Reprinted 2013

Table of Contents

Foreword

Looking back in my 26 years in education, I can't think of a time when a book like this was needed more. Increasingly, we struggle to teach more in less time, prepare students for tests we often find not useful or descriptive, and stay on top of the field by reading new professional titles and research—and we do it all alone. We earnestly seek to improve our teaching practice, but discover how difficult it is to reflect on teaching when we're so busy just doing it! When we seek another colleague's perspective, we find that we can't even have lunch with her—her students are already back in class when ours go to lunch. I can think of no other field with as little built-in collaboration time as teaching. As so many others have noted, it's easy to understand why so many teachers feel quite isolated.

Fortunately, thousands of schools around the country have taken the important step to provide school-based literacy coaches who promote improved teaching and learning by collaborating with colleagues. We have abundant evidence that, if coaches and teachers collaborate effectively, we can expect to realize those goals. However, the manner in which districts have defined these new roles and laid out plans for effective interaction between teachers and coaches varies widely. In some schools, coaches play quasi-administrative roles, supervising the lunchroom, administering tests, and covering classrooms when there are no substitutes. In others, classroom teachers are reluctant to work with a coach, possibly because they have mistaken the role of a coach and wonder if they really serve as an evaluator. Teachers are left wondering exactly how to interact with coaches who may, very recently, have been their own classroom teaching colleagues.

In the just-in-time category, Cheryl Jones and Mary Vreeman have written a wonderful book that charts a course to collaboration for instructional coaches and classroom teachers. They have shown the way out of isolation and into the kind of professional growth that can only be realized by working in a collaborative relationship with a knowledgeable colleague. In *Instructional*

Coaches and Classroom Teachers: Sharing the Road to Success, Mary and Cheryl lay out, in the most practical way imaginable, exactly why collaborating with a coach works and exactly what characterizes successful coaching relationships. This is no small feat, given the demands on professionals in both roles.

Building on years of successes and challenges in providing support for teachers in Hillsborough County, Florida, Cheryl and Mary tackle a very ambitious agenda in this book. They explore not only the compelling case for collaboration, but go on to clearly articulate appropriate roles for classroom teachers and coaches; this serves to dispel some common myths about coaching and to outline different ways of working together throughout a teacher's career span and in a wide variety of school contexts.

This book is written from the perspective of the classroom teacher—something that others who have written about coaching have neglected to consider. Cheryl and Mary tackle questions that will come from teachers who are already very skilled, as well as those just beginning to teach: Why should I work with a coach? How will my existing expertise and beliefs be acknowledged? How will our collaboration matter for students' learning? They examine how to overcome barriers that may prevent successful working relationships and how different contexts and circumstances should alter the collaborative relationship. This book about why and how classroom teachers can benefit from coaching becomes a superb treatise on how to coach well.

In a conversational style, imbued with wonderful anecdotes and stories from numerous classroom teachers, as well as learning experiences gathered at the authors' own dinner tables, we get to accompany the teachers with whom Mary and Cheryl have worked on a journey of collaboration that ultimately benefits students. They share, in an unflinchingly honest way, how coaching has succeeded and when the process has faltered. The authors ask us to engage in numerous moments of reflection in which we explore our own beliefs and practices and, in doing so, consider ways to apply what we know about students' learning to our own lives.

It is difficult to interact with colleagues in this era of growing demands on teachers. It seems that everyone *but* the classroom teacher is making decisions for the classroom teacher. Too often, professional learning is offered as a one-size-fits-all inservice that meets the needs of less than 10 percent of those attending. That's the bad news.

The good—no, great—news is that teachers and coaches, collaborating on behalf of students, are reclaiming the decision-making process and are customizing professional learning, classroom by classroom. In a highly readable and straightforward way, Cheryl and Mary have written what would have taken us years to discover on our own—how to make these relationships most productive and beneficial to children. Coaching is a means to that end, as it is student learning we care most about. It is on that common ground that they suggest we begin to open ourselves to what may well become the most significant relationships of our professional lives.

Ellin Oliver Keene, M.A.

Preface

As you traverse a path of self-directed learning and renewal, we hope our book will provide answers to many of your questions. Why would I work with a coach? This is a question that many teachers ask. We offer answers to this question throughout our book. As teachers and coaches ourselves, we believe you should tap the services of a coach because you deserve to be recognized, supported, celebrated, understood, and valued for answering a sacred call—the call to teach.

We have written *Instructional Coaches and Classroom Teachers: Sharing the Road to Success* with the heart and soul of the classroom teacher in mind. It is you who light the way for tomorrow's leaders and citizens. In this book, we want to herald you who work where the action is. As new education policies and related mandates continue to be delivered, we recognize that it is the teachers who must ensure that policies implemented are in the best interests of children. Making sure that policies do indeed serve children—rather than children being used to serve the policies—is a challenge facing all of us in education. We believe that in order for teachers to stay true to the purposes of the profession, they should allow themselves the privilege of support and help. We suggest that there is no need for teachers to attempt to go it alone. We invite you to reach out and grow in the company of others—coaches and colleagues.

In writing this book, we operate from the perspectives of both teacher and coach. Together we have 34 years of cumulative teaching and coaching service in the school district of Hillsborough County, Florida, the eighth-largest school district in the nation. This district offers us diverse and rich experiences in school communities that represent a range from affluence to poverty. (Poverty rates in the district schools range from a high of 98 percent to a low of 6 percent.) The schools also vary in setting—inner city, urban, suburban, and rural. Many schools experience high rates of student mobility. We find that schools with high student mobility also often experience high teacher turnover. These factors in combination increase the challenges for both teachers and coaches.

We share this information to encourage you as you read this book. We do not come from a place far off and distant from the classroom. We have encountered the same challenges you face as teachers and coaches. As teachers, we have felt the need to tap the collective wisdom of our colleagues when a designated coach was not available to us. As coaches, we have had the privilege of working with many teachers, supporting them in areas they defined, so that together we could develop learning environments and opportunities that met the diverse needs of the students.

We hope that this book will spark interest and provide inspiration for classroom teachers to investigate the benefits that coaching can offer both personally and professionally. Just as importantly, we hope to reveal the impact working with a coach can have on the students you teach.

We issue an invitation to all who are looking to empower themselves to think and practice their way to better teaching. We urge you to step inside a new way of thinking and doing, in the company of others. A problem we face in our schools is that our students differ in many ways, and their needs may not neatly align with the demands of mandates, prescriptive programs, and reform initiatives. We realize there is no simple one-size-fits-all solution. May we have the courage to open ourselves to others so that *we* may grow as we help our students grow.

We believe that the heart of a teacher beats with the desire to answer the call to teaching in such a way that we can always look back in satisfaction to a job well done. We hope this book will not only help you look back in satisfaction but realize that at each step of your journey you said yes to being more than you ever imagined you could be for your students. Please join us as we share how we came to coaching and what we have learned along the way—*where the rubber hits the road.*

Cheryl Jones, M.Ed. and Mary Vreeman, M.A.

Acknowledgements

To the *School Board of Hillsborough County Public Schools,* we express our gratitude for the visionary leadership in their ongoing support for coaching. We thank *Dr. Earl J. Lennard,* former superintendent of Hillsborough County Schools, for his willingness to embrace and advocate for our coaching project. Thanks to *Superintendent Mary Ellen Elia* for her passion for supporting classrooms through coaching. We thank *Dr. Michael Grego* for his ongoing support for coaching. To *Dr. Joyce Haines,* we express our thanks for helping us remain on a path to realizing the true benefit of coaching—your knowledge and understanding, as well as your tireless efforts to keep our project alive, are most appreciated. We owe tremendous thanks to *Dr. Grace Albritton* for her feedback and recommendations. Thanks to *Barbara Hancock* for continuing her work with us so that every classroom will have the support of a coach. To *Pam Locke,* thank you for paving the path for our coaching leaders. To *Susan Avery* and *Mellissa Alonso,* thank you for an idea that continues to have a great impact on teachers and students in our district. You have led us to new ways of thinking and doing.

We say thank you to our many experts who have provided insight and guidance—*Brenda Parkes, Stephanie Harvey, Pam Robbins,* and *Jim Knight.* A special thanks to *Steve Barkley,* who has been a powerful guiding light in helping our project grow. A special note of gratitude goes to the members of our reading team: *Glenda Brown, Cristie Mosblech, Angela Butler, Melissa Izzo, Debbie Anderson,* and *Tracy Crothers.* And thanks to our wonderful *Zoila Araujo-Ferrer* for her hard work and patience.

We also thank those who had a direct impact on the writing of this book. Thanks go to *Carol York* for her encouragement, mentoring, and guidance. *Joan Irwin,* our amazing editor, has remained in tune with our heads and our hearts each step of the way. Thanks to *Jeff Brake,* who has been a partner and friend in this endeavor.

To *Ellin Keene*—we simply say WOW! You continue to humble, inspire, and empower us to lead the force to impact education in a way that will truly serve our children.

Cheryl's acknowledgements: Numerous colleagues and friends helped me find my path to coaching: *Betty Hartwick*, an inspiration both in and out of the classroom; *Mary Garced, Ed Rehmeyer, Ellen Oberschall*, and *Joann Shaw*, who coached me before we even knew what coaching was; *Pam Tompkins*, thanks for mentoring me and nudging me to take that first step into formal coaching; *Lynn Rattray*, who taught me about leadership; *Peggy Eakins*, who always knows when I need to be taken under her wing; *Pam Locke* for her brilliant thoughts and vision; *Joani Altshuler*, thanks for patiently teaching me so much. *Jan Segal*, my mentor and friend; *Shelley*, my best buddy who knows how to help through the hard times and does cartwheels to celebrate the good times; and to my incredible writing partner, *Mary*, thanks for the way you truly "get me" and for knowing how to nudge me into action from my "paralysis by analysis." To my first teachers, my parents, I am most thankful. Thanks also to my big sister *Cindy*, my first mentor and coach! I am most thankful for my children, *Kyle, Curt*, and *Emily*, who teach me the most sacred lessons of all. And to my husband, *Doug*: You are always and ever still the amazing man I married. I couldn't be me and do what I do without your love and support.

Mary's acknowledgements: Thank you to my colleagues at West Tampa Elementary and Morgan Woods Elementary who made it their mission each day to collaborate, plan, and help each other. They were my first peer coaches. Thank you to my partner in writing this book, as well as the person sharing the highs and lows of our educational journey together: *Cheryl Jones*. She has been such a profound influence on me and has truly been my coach over the last decade. I come from a family of teachers and professors who are madly in love with the idea that *using* the knowledge you acquire exceeds the value of carrying it around in your head. My mother constantly coached my creative side, while my father worked tirelessly to instill a work ethic that would serve me well. They recognized my strengths and encouraged me to run with them. Last but not least, my husband, *John*. He has reminded me to keep my life in balance. Thank you, "Nhoj," for giving up your time for me and recognizing the importance of the work that we continue to be passionate about—and hopefully always will be!

Introduction

Instructional Coaches and Classroom Teachers: Sharing the Road to Success is written from the perspective of classroom teachers—not coaches, not district leaders, not school administrators, not curriculum consultants, and not any other specialists whose views are widely represented in other books about coaching. This book is for all teachers who wish to take a step forward in examining their teaching and improving their practice. This book attempts to address the fears, feelings, and misconceptions that often hinder teachers from working effectively with coaches. We hope the messages of inspiration and practical realities contained in these pages will be just what you are looking for as you embark on coaching activities. We have used a road metaphor to frame our message in a way that will help you see yourself as the driver, the navigator, the one in charge of your professional learning experiences.

Traveling the road to success in coaching involves paying attention to a variety of signposts that indicate ways in which teachers and coaches can work together. The signposts we have chosen include research findings that reveal the benefits of coaching, personal stories and examples based on realities of the classroom, humorous vignettes about teaching and life, and the voices of teachers helping other teachers to identify needs and overcome fears about, as well as possible hesitation or reluctance to participate in, coaching activities. We have attempted to share a myriad of options and opportunities that put you in the driver's seat. From this position you can determine the direction you might choose for coaching your way to improved practice and rewarding results. Now let's look at what you will encounter as you make your way through *Instructional Coaches and Classroom Teachers: Sharing the Road to Success*.

Chapter One: Starting Down the Yellow Brick Road

Teaching is an *enormous* undertaking—one that is far too tough to attempt alone. Working together, teachers and coaches can address the challenges they share in this age of accountability and high-stakes tests. Our purpose in this chapter is to demonstrate the benefits that come from working in the company of colleagues. There are several signposts that will help you realize certain truths and principles about coaching. We point to the difficulties of taking an ideal vision into daily practice to help you appreciate why it is often so hard to *make happen* what we want to *have happen* in our classrooms.

Coaching is a two-way street for inspiration—you will find you receive inspiration from, as well as provide inspiration for, those you partner with in coaching activities. Coaching does not entertain any notions of perfection, performance, or evaluation. The focus of coaching activities is not to render judgment but rather to develop powerful communication among educators that enables them to capture and share a common vision for improving student achievement.

The first chapter of *Instructional Coaches and Classroom Teachers: Sharing the Road to Success* provides the rationale and reasons for you to design a path for your professional growth through coaching activities. In writing this and the other chapters of this book, we hope to provide a helpful tool that is written with the heart and soul of the teacher in mind. We write for teachers who deserve the same support that our star athletes and performers enjoy—teachers deserve the support of a coach!

Chapter Two: Taking the Road Less Traveled

This chapter is a call for courage—courage to be *all* you can be when making changes in your teaching. Knowing how hard it is to make changes midstream, we present a reality-based approach to coaching. In this chapter, we identify many of the stumbling blocks to overcome in order to embrace coaching. We want to help you take the steps to develop your own program for self-reflection and growth.

By the time you complete this chapter, you will have reflected on your current progress and realized what may be holding you back from further advancements with coaching. You will be ready to commit your ability to take the risks necessary to be coached.

Chapter Three: Recognizing Detours and Dead Ends

Misconceptions about coaching abound and can thus fuel fears about working with coaches. In this chapter we drive straight through these misunderstandings by identifying several myths and realities about coaching. As you read this chapter, you will encounter some familiar beliefs that are actually misconceptions about coaching. Our discussion is intended to help you form a clear vision for coaching that will enable you to develop your own plan for working with a coach. This vision will help you see the latitude that exists among choices of activities for coaching. You will see that coaches, while working with teachers, are also learning and growing professionally. A coach learns with and from you. Coaching builds upon the power of collaboration and provides opportunities to explore and examine our beliefs in the company of others. Reading this chapter will enhance your understanding of how coaching can help you connect your teaching ideals with the reality of day-to-day activities in your classroom.

Chapter Four: Sharing the Driving

Relationships are at the heart of coaching. In this chapter you will find many suggestions for and examples of collaborative efforts, all of which are centered on teacher-coach cooperation. We explore ways in which you can use the services of a coach and demonstrate the value of having a trusted companion (a coach) along as you navigate your teaching career. We suggest that you begin to devise a plan that identifies which areas of your professional experience merit coaching. This plan is a practical tool that defines who will be responsible for specific coaching components and activities. Notably, we provide a picture of coaching as on-site and job-embedded support designed to meet your specific needs. This view will enable you to deepen your professional relationships and interactions with peers. With this understanding of coaching, you will likely discover that you have acquired a renewed ability to honestly appraise your current instructional methods by recognizing your areas of strength and courageously identifying areas in which to grow.

Chapter Five: Finding Rewards in Twists and Turns

Coaching offers something for every teacher—from the beginner to the seasoned veteran. In this chapter we explore universal actions in which all teachers engage during the coaching process, as well as show how coaching functions at different stages of a teaching career. For preservice teachers, this material will foreshadow what you may encounter when you begin teaching and help you prepare for those new experiences. Beginning teachers will find support and encouragement to face the reality of the challenges that can threaten to extinguish their visions. Experienced teachers will be reminded of familiar situations with different perspectives to approach in new ways through coaching activities. Though we may be at different points in our journey, working in the company of a coach or colleague can light our way to powerful and purposeful practice. As you reflect on places visited and preview places yet to come, you will realize how continuous dialogue with peers can help you look at the place where you have arrived, assess where you want to now go, and understand that through coaching you can embrace the changes you need to make in order to reach your destination.

Chapter Six: Slowing Down to Speed Up

As we work amid mounting pressures and demands, it is easy to get caught in the busyness of our work and miss the critical targets we initially aimed to accomplish. This chapter will meet you where you operate daily to remind you to stay true to your mission—to provide the best possible instruction for your students. For example, we offer guidance in examining classroom routines and reflecting on attempts at implementing new strategies that are not initially successful. In each case, time is a crucial element—learning and change both take time.

Through your work with coaching, you can take the time to reflect on what is happening as a result of your teaching efforts. You will be encouraged to take time to recognize and celebrate your successes. You can feel renewed by finding ways to embrace the personal rewards you gain from the success of your students.

By learning how to "slow down to speed up," you will begin to effectively pace yourself with realistic yet commendable goals.

Chapter Seven: Navigating Your Own Coaching Path

So what do you do if you have no designated coach at your school? Answers to that very question can be found in Chapter Seven. This chapter also provides new ideas for *every* teacher, regardless of your situation. We offer guidelines that will help you identify opportunities for coaching partnerships that exist in every school. We have provided many avenues and ideas for how you might engage with your professional peers to provide coaching experiences.

Chapter Eight: Taking the High Road

We close the book with some guidelines to keep you on a path that will realize the benefits and rewards of coaching. Working in the company of your peers will lead to enhanced professional awareness. In this chapter we remind you that coaching serves to identify strengths, as well as opportunities for growth. Remember to maintain a balance in your focus as you examine your practice. As you work through one process of change after another, you will begin to accumulate increased self-awareness and self-confidence in your ability to navigate your path to excellence!

Features of *Instructional Coaches and Classroom Teachers: Sharing the Road to Success*

We know that teachers have busy lives, so we have included some features that we hope will make our book reader friendly.

- "Thoughts About Coaching" summarize core ideas that are developed in each chapter.
- Vignettes and personal stories frame our work in the realities of life both in and out of school.
- Teacher voices provide authenticity and great insights born of individual coaching experiences.
- Quotations offer thought-provoking messages about coaching, teaching, and learning.

- Research evidence and the voices of experts establish the credibility of our work.
- "Reflection" invites you to explore your thoughts about coaching and helps you begin to pave a path for professional growth.
- Appendices offer a range of resources to support your coaching activities.

Throughout the book, we have tried to capture a realistic perspective of teaching and coaching for our readers. We realize that none of us operates in a vacuum but must navigate endless demands while also embracing different ideologies, learning styles, and personalities of peers and our students.

Suggestions for Using *Instructional Coaches and Classroom Teachers: Sharing the Road to Success*

We wrote this book to provide a clear picture of the role that teachers have in coaching activities. Our wish is that you will use this book for professional and personal growth. As you read *Instructional Coaches and Classroom Teachers: Sharing the Road to Success*, you will find many avenues to explore as you look for ways to improve your current practices and take advantage of opportunities to work collaboratively with peers. These experiences can lead to deepened reflections and growth in your knowledge of teaching and learning. You may choose to share the book and the subsequent learning with a peer, or you may see yourself as the leader of a book-study group for your grade level or school community. You may choose to explore only the section that pertains to you in the here and now.

We see this book as a resource for teachers, coaches, administrators, and district leaders who wish to delve into issues that confront coaching and develop strategies that will enable them to move forward more effectively with their teachers. This book provides a vehicle not only for understanding what coaching offers but also in helping you create a culture of coaching at your school.

Starting Down the Yellow Brick Road

Thoughts About Coaching

- Coaching is about communication.
- Coaching is about sharing visions to improve student achievement.
- Coaching is about the desire to be inspired and to be inspiring.
- Coaching is about professional growth—not performance, supervision, or evaluation.

Some Observations About Teaching and Coaching

A teacher was standing in front of his class sharing the exciting news that he had been contacted by the local TV station. The station wanted to do a story about teachers who go above and beyond their duties to make learning come alive for their students. He explained that the story would cover the field trip he had planned for the class. He began to expound on the details of their upcoming trip to the zoo. He was recounting an exhaustive list of preparations he had completed to ensure the outing was educational as well as a memorable once-in-a-lifetime event. His enthusiasm was inspired by the intense effort he had put into each and every detail. He shared with his students a schedule for the day that included an exciting tour of the zoo guided by a world-renowned expert, an opportunity to assist the zookeeper in caring for and feeding the animals, and eating lunch in the aviary. As he came to a close, he waited expectantly for a response. As the class remained silent, a voice in the back said, "Yeah, but what's in it for us?"

Can you relate to this scenario? As teachers, we are often frustrated when students seem to miss the point and purpose of our efforts, which is to serve them in ways that are beneficial to them. However, they have to be willing learners for the actions we take to move them to a desired outcome. A willing learner has to be able to answer the compelling question, "What's in it for me?"

Coaches, like teachers, have similar experiences. Many teachers operate with this same query when confronted with opportunities to work with a coach. Teachers want to see the purpose and point of it all. With no time or energy to spare, they want answers to "What's in it for me?" This is an important question to consider before any effective work with a coach can begin. By effective work we mean work that will result in profit and gain for both students and teachers.

The vignette on page 19 illustrates the hard work and effort that teachers contribute in order to make their instruction meaningful, even though it goes unrecognized by the students. This also occurs with coaches. They spend endless hours preparing, reading, researching, and practicing new ideas before entering into a coaching relationship with fellow educators. But we know that regardless of their efforts, the question "What's in it for me?" still needs to be answered. This question is one that both teacher and coach need to consider.

Let's begin to answer that question by relating it to a condition we all experience in our schools today—stress over testing. It seems that an enormous amount of our time with students is spent administering test after test after test. It is easy to become so involved with meeting deadlines for mandated testing and reporting that we ignore the real benefit that can be reaped from these assessments. The real and true purpose for testing is not to render judgment, but rather to seek information that will assist us in serving our students. However, the real purpose can get lost in the task if we fail to retrieve what's in it for teachers and students.

Test Anxiety: A Coach's Story

Allow us to share a story that one of our coaches, Mary Kelley, shared with us. Many of the schools in our district are part of a Reading First Grant. One of the grant requirements is to test children three to four times each year with DIBELS® (Dynamic Indicators of Basic Early Literacy Skills) assessments to screen students for risk level and for progress-monitoring purposes. Mary was administering the Nonsense Word Fluency test to kindergartners. One little boy sat down to be tested, looking morose and sad. When Mary attempted to diffuse his anxiety, he told her he needed to share something really bad with her. She replied she would be happy to let him share anything he wanted. He leaned in close and put his hand against his face to shield his words from going anywhere except directly into her ear. With a little lisp he reported, "Sometimes I get my *b*'s and *d*'s mixed up." Mary smiled and giggled and shared back in a dramatic whisper, "That's okay. Sometimes I do, too!" He looked at her with grave surprise and asked, "Is that okay?" She nodded and shared that she was still learning, too. She just needed to see what he already knew so his teacher would know what to teach him next. He smiled a grateful smile, and they began the task of testing. When he came to the word *dak*, he pronounced with great confidence, "dak!" and then quickly looked up with questioning eyes and said, or "bak?"

Isn't the little guy in our story adorable? We bet you have no problem relating to that situation. We all agree with the importance of clearly communicating the purpose of testing to our students. We want them to believe and understand that we do not expect perfection. We only expect an honest effort that will help us determine a plan of action that will meet their specific needs.

Student anxiety over test performance is a direct parallel to the anxiety most teachers experience about coaching. You may at times feel just like the boy in the story we shared. You may be thinking that you must be perfect before sharing your teaching skills with a coworker. This is a huge misconception. Coaching is *not* about performance. It is instead about professional study and growth. The purpose of coaching is exactly the same purpose we have for serving our children. In coached lessons, the goal is for honest reflection that will help determine the next steps in our growth and development as teachers.

Think of coaching as your own private access to action research—research you get to design, implement, and use as you see fit to achieve what *you* desire for your classroom. We will address this and other prevalent misconceptions about coaching in Chapter Three. Feel free to skip to that chapter now if you must—if not, let's embark on a journey of discovering why coaching is exactly what you have been seeking your entire teaching career. Let's begin by sharing a bit of fun.

A friend of mine had just described his vacation experiences.

"It sounds as if you had a great time in Texas," I observed. "But didn't you tell me you were planning to visit Colorado?"

"Well, we changed our plans because, uh…"

His wife cut in, "Oh tell the truth, Fred!" He fell silent and she continued, "You know, it's just ridiculous. Fred simply will not ask for directions!" (Morgan 1981, 54)

Sound silly? Of course it does. But may we be reminded of how easy it is to recognize the folly of others while our own folly remains hidden from our conscious view. As educators, we also lose our way. Our illustration serves an important purpose. We all agree that we have a definite place where we want to arrive with our students. Though there may be more than one way to travel, we must be careful that we stay on a course that will in fact lead us to our desired destination. We need a map, yes, but we also need outside help to read our map and apply it to our navigational skills (teaching). We need help to ensure that we are traveling the *best* route possible to our destination. This book is designed to help you find the support you need in order to arrive at your desired destination feeling *fully* alive, healthy, and satisfied!

"Teaching is too tough to go it alone," writes Regie Routman (2000, xlii). Anyone out there agree that teaching is tough? It *is* tough and seems to gets tougher each year.

Teachers and Lawyers: Cheryl's Story

I recently met a friend of my husband who was formerly a teacher. He returned to law school and now works for a prestigious law firm. This firm is known for riding its attorneys for every minute of life it can get from them. When he found out I was a teacher, he literally bowed to me. He turned to his colleague and said, "You know, as hard as we work, I have never worked harder than when I was a teacher!"

We *do* work hard! How many times have you felt bewildered, overwhelmed, and alone in your efforts to surmount the endless tasks of teaching? You work tirelessly and yet often feel you fail miserably in meeting the needs of your students. Do you ever feel scared—like you're the only one who doesn't know how to do this all perfectly? Do you ever wonder what is wrong with you as you watch colleagues arrive and leave on time while your day stretches hours beyond what you are paid to work?

This is what this book is all about—recognizing what we *all* feel, fear, and often try to hide inside. This job—this calling, this profession—is bigger than we ever dreamed it would be. It is in fact bigger than all of us. We need the help and companionship of others to navigate the increasingly complex profession called teaching. "We read so we know we are not alone," wrote a student of C.S. Lewis in the movie *Shadowlands* (1993). Many of us do feel alone in our fears and frustrations. Might we be so bold as to suggest that a direct benefit of coaching is to know you are *not* alone? Isn't it a comfort to know there is someone willing to walk with us, learn with us, struggle with us, and celebrate with us? We can learn much—if we are open to it—from the wisdom of others. We can come to learn in new ways and strengthen and revitalize our teaching (Routman 1996). If you ever find the going too tough to go it alone, then this book is for you.

Okay—so maybe we have your attention. You agree, but so what? How can a book change anything? You are so right! A book, a program, a mandate might pose reasons or requirements for doing certain things, but that is not what drives us to embrace the need for growth and change. We may go through the motions of changing practice, but if we see no real purpose for our students or ourselves, it will be just that—meaningless motions.

This story comes to us through oral tradition. Imagine the following scene:

A mother is in the kitchen preparing the traditional ham dinner for a family gathering. Her young daughter is looking on as she works. The mother carefully slices off one end of the ham. The daughter asks, "Mommy, why do you have to cut the end of the ham like that?" The mother replies, "I learned how to cook a ham from your aunt, and that is the way she always did it."

"Oh, I see," says the daughter.

The next day at the family gathering, the daughter saw her aunt and asked, "Auntie, why do you have to cut the end of the ham off before you cook it?"

The aunt responded, "I learned to cook from your grandmother and that's the way she always did it."

Can you guess what happens next? You got it. The girl's grandmother arrives, so she implores in the same manner, "Grandma, why do you have to cut the end of the ham off before you cook it?" Looking puzzled, the grandmother looks around the room at her daughters and granddaughter. The aunt speaks up and says, "You know, Mom… how you taught me to always cut off the end of the ham when you were cooking a big ham for our family gatherings." The grandmother smiled sheepishly and said, "Well I don't know why you do it, but I always had to do it because my pan was too short!"

We laugh at this mindless mimicry, but don't we all fall prey to similar behaviors? In the day-to-day pressures, we often find ourselves going through similar motions of empty practice. We want to help you move beyond mindless motions to purposeful practice, help you embrace what you do each day with a true commitment of mind, heart, and soul, and help you find your way to a practice of teaching that will rekindle your passion for what you do. Isn't it time to recapture the vision you held when you first made the sacred commitment to enter the classroom? Let's start the journey to that very destination now.

Mapping Our Way to Coaching

The first step we must take in order to operate at the mind, heart, and soul level of teaching is to have confidence that what we are doing will in fact create the desired positive change in our students. It is the teaching with purpose that will make the difference. Without a clear purpose, you have no foundation on which to base your decisions, allocate your time, and use your resources. You will tend to make choices based on circumstances, pressures, and your mood at that moment. People who don't know their purpose try to do too much, and that causes stress, fatigue, and conflict (Warren 2002).

Does any of this have a familiar ring? It's not that teachers aren't willing to work hard. It's not that teachers aren't willing to do enough. We believe teachers *are* willing to change their practices when they can see that it benefits their students. We believe it is every teacher's desire to see each day as a day of reckoning where we reconcile our actions with the desired end results. It is our ability to maintain *this* vision for success that will move us to refine and revise practice appropriately. However, desire is not enough—we must transform the desire into action. Are you with us so far?

Reflection

Take a moment to jot down some notes in a journal about what you may be thinking and feeling so far. You can use these thoughts to guide you later.

Okay, so we may have the desire to change, and we realize we need to take action. This, folks, is where the proverbial rubber hits the road. Schmoker observes, "The problem is not that we do not know enough—it is that we do not *do what we already know.* We do not act on or refine or apply those principles and practices that *virtually every teacher already* knows" (2005, 148). So why don't we *do* what we know? Because it simply isn't that easy—that's why!

Has this ever happened to you? You go to a workshop and the trainers provide some terrific new ways of teaching that excite you. They cite the research that supports their training and you heartily agree. You agree because you see the evidence of that research in your students every day! You get all fired up and determine you will turn a new leaf—add a new dimension to your teaching. Your enthusiasm grows as your thoughts, beliefs, and feelings converge together in agreement with what is presented. You leave the workshop full of inspiration and conviction for what you will do differently with your students. Then something happens on your way back to the classroom that causes you to forget your new convictions and passion. Or, you actually make it back to your classroom with these passionate convictions and plans intact, but something happens as you try to put those plans into action. You believe it *could* make a difference, but now you don't know how in the world to begin. How do you change your classroom instruction and routines to support what you want to do? How can you possibly add one more thing to an already overstuffed day? What will you remove? How will you get this to actually work with the diverse and challenging group of kids sitting before you? You may find yourself giving up before you even get started. Or, you may take that courageous leap but somehow what you imagined would happen with your kids is not at all what plays out in your first attempts. You give up, thinking that either you are not capable, your students are not capable, or perhaps both. Discouraging, isn't it? After a few experiences like this, you may give up completely. In fact, you just might become so jaded that you can no longer embrace new ideas even at the knowledge or thought level.

You are not alone in this dilemma of heart, mind, and spirit. We can agree with research and have a burning desire to change, but the knowing and agreeing (though necessary) are not sufficient to make the intended change. It is the "how to do it" that trips us up, frustrates us, and, more often than not, chases us back to our old and familiar ways.

We believe that working with a coach is an obvious solution to this dilemma. This concept of coaching seems to be reaching mass proportions today. We have worked with our coaching project since 1999. We continue to reflect and ponder how we can make our project truly serve the intended end users— teachers. As we have wrestled with this issue, we have read books and articles and read even *more* books and articles. We have come to a startling realization along the way. All the books we find are written to the audience of coaches or those who would administrate a coaching initiative. We think the most important audience has been left out of the loop—the teachers! In discussing the idea of writing a book, we agreed on one condition—that it would be written for teachers. We are part of a growing chorus of writers who recognize the critical role for teachers in professional learning activities (Darling-Hammond 1997; DuFour 2005; Little 1990, 2007; Lortie 1975; Schmoker 2005). For example, Schmoker notes, "Teachers do not learn best from outside experts or by attending conferences or implementing 'programs' installed by outsiders. Teachers learn best from other teachers, in settings where they literally teach each other the art of teaching" (2005, 141).

Although we believe coaching *is* a viable vehicle, we also realize it is still an oft-misunderstood and mistrusted concept. We find it interesting that in the sports and entertainment fields, it is accepted practice to hire the best coach money can buy in order to take individuals to the maximum level of performance. Athletes and performers *expect* coaching to be part of a successful career path. Isn't it about time that teachers expect this and even demand this for themselves as well? Isn't it ridiculous to think that this critical support would only be made available to those who are charged with entertaining us, while ignoring the needs of those in charge of our very future? We hope our time together in this book will help move teachers from fearing what coaching might do *to* them to discovering the possibilities and power coaching offers *for* them. We hope to leave you wondering how anyone could think it possible to ever be without a coach!

> *"One of the beauties of teaching is that there is no limit to one's growth as a teacher, just as there is no knowing beforehand how much your students can learn."*
>
> —*Herbert Kohl*

What Coaching Can Do for You

Let's start our work together by helping you answer the important question of "What's in it for me?" Since we know the dangers of relying on mere opinion, let's start with some research that will hopefully begin to build your level of confidence in this thing called coaching. Our coaching project began as a response to a requirement to increase districtwide efforts to meet the needs of struggling readers in K–2 classrooms. Many options and plan designs were considered, but the research of Joyce and Showers prompted our district to move in a new direction (1988; 2002). Their research indicated that coached support was necessary to ensure that teachers implemented new curriculum and teaching models into general practice and thereby influenced students' learning environments (Joyce and Showers 1988). Sound familiar? This research focused on the experience we just discussed about the difficulties of taking new information from training into the classroom where it can actually work to positively impact student achievement.

The research of Joyce and Showers reveals that it takes greater support than the traditional "sit and get" workshop to implement changes. Some of these findings are summarized in Table 1.1. Let's take a look at what this research reveals.

Table 1.1 Teacher Effectiveness Steps

Training Steps	Knowledge Mastery (%)	Skill Acquisition (%)	On-the-Job Application (%)
Theory	Middle to High 85	Low 15	Very low 5–10
Theory and Demonstration	High 85	Low to Middle 18	Very Low 5–10
Theory, Demonstration, and Practice/Feedback	High 85	High 85	Very Low 10–15
Theory, Demonstration, Practice/Feedback, and Coaching	High 90	High 90	High 80–90

Based on Joyce, B., and B. Showers. 2002. *Student achievement through staff development*. 3rd ed. Alexandria, VA: Association for Supervision & Curriculum Development.

Table 1.1 clearly illustrates that when teachers attend a presentation that only delivers theory, their knowledge may grow, but the new knowledge does not increase their skills and has minimal application in the classroom. When staff developers add demonstration or modeling during the training session, teachers are able to implement new knowledge and skill at the workshop, but very seldom transfer the new knowledge and skill to their classroom practice. When teachers are allowed time to actually practice and receive immediate feedback from trainers and peers during the training session, the skill level of the teacher grows dramatically. However, the skill level still does not transfer to any significant degree in their classroom. The researchers found that the key to realizing successful use of new knowledge and skills in the classroom is the support of a colleague (a coach) in the classroom setting. By working with a coach when implementing new practices, the teacher has the opportunity to see it modeled in their particular classroom with all the realities and challenges that face them each day. It is at this point that attending training actually makes a difference for the students.

Reflection

Take a few minutes to think about issues you have faced when trying to implement new skills, strategies, and methods you acquired in a workshop training model. How does your experience compare to the aspects of effectiveness shown in Table 1.1?

Coaching Results in One School District

The School District of Hillsborough County, where we have both worked as teachers and coaches, instituted a program of on-site staff development in 64 elementary schools and two early-childhood centers. The program was in place throughout 2000–2001 and continues today. Thirty-two K–2 reading coaches served these schools, as well as two other reading coaches who worked in an additional four schools for part of the year. Each reading coach was typically assigned to two elementary schools geographically close to one another; the two principals collaborated in selecting the reading coach.

During 2000–2001, the district conducted an evaluation of the impact of the coaching project on student reading achievement. After one year of implementing the K–2 Reading Coach Project in schools with highest need, we were able to obtain evidence that the support of a coach had a positive effect on student achievement (Albritton 2001). The evaluation used two complementary achievement tests: the Developmental Reading Assessment (DRA), a criterion-referenced test, and the Stanford Achievement Test, 9th Edition (Stanford-9), which is the district's norm-referenced achievement test. Existing test data primarily required for evaluation of the Title VI Class Size Reduction (CSR) program were also used. It is noteworthy that considerable overlap exists between CSR sites and schools served by the K–2 reading coaches.

At the first-grade level, students typically performed at kindergarten or early preprimer instructional reading levels on the pre-test DRA in the fall of 2000. By spring 2001, the scores were distributed so as to resemble a normal curve ranging from zero to 44 (fifth-grade level) with the most frequent score at level 18 (early second grade). The same pattern of low levels of achievement on the DRA pretest and widely distributed levels of achievement on the post-test held up for all ethnic groups, for boys and girls, and for Limited English Proficiency (LEP) students. Similarly, a wide range of achievement on the post-test was evident at all sites where the DRA was administered.

Similar findings were evident in the results from the Stanford-9 administered in the first and second grades. At the first-grade level, 5,651 students in 61 schools with K–2 reading coaches and a free/reduced-price lunch eligibility rate of 69.7 percent attained scores comparable to average students in the nation. Similar results were found with students in the second grade.

Based on this evidence, the district recommended continuing the K–2 Reading Coaches Initiative and, when possible, expanding the number of schools assigned a reading coach. Additional recommendations related to continued administration of the DRA and the Stanford-9 as part of the evaluation of the Reading Coaches Initiative. There was also consideration of how to use the DRA more widely throughout the district by determining what other personnel could be trained to use the assessment in schools where no reading coach was assigned.

Moving Ahead on the Yellow Brick Road

Still not convinced you should work with a coach? Maybe we can help you think differently by using an analogy most people can easily relate to. Many of you either have experienced or will come to a time in your life when you will be responsible for teaching a teenager to drive.

Teaching My Daughter to Drive: Cheryl's Story

When my daughter, Emily, was ready to drive, much had been learned from the experience of teaching my two sons, Kyle and Curt. I decided we would really do it right this time. The teacher/coach in me would not allow me to repeat my past failed attempts with my older children. After much reflection, I decided to follow the model for teaching I used in my classroom. The model of I do/We do/You do became a focus for how we would approach the fearsome task before us. The first thing I did differently was to have Emily start watching me as I drove. The radio was silenced and she had to endure lengthy and detailed explanations of my ongoing thinking process when driving. (As you can imagine, she just loved this!) Once satisfied that she understood the thinking process, my husband, Doug, took her to the parking lot of her high school for her first experience behind the wheel. We wanted her to get comfortable with the car and how it functions without any distractions. Once she knew how to stop, start, and turn in isolation from other factors, we began to let her practice on roads. These first trials of driving occurred in our neighborhood. She eventually became very efficient and confident in this protected and mild setting. Now, wouldn't you think we were insane if we withdrew our support at this point? Think how dangerous it would have been for her (and all of you out on the road as well) if we had said, "Emily, you are doing a great job in the parking lot and an adequate job in the neighborhood. We know you will someday want to go other places, and there are highways, freeways, and interstates that will take you anywhere you want to go. So good luck, sweetie!" How silly it would be to withdraw our support at the point when it was needed most.

Think of learning new strategies and techniques for teaching in the same manner as Emily learning to drive a car. The workshop setting is your parking lot and neighborhood driving experience. It is devoid of the realities of teaching. When you attempt to implement the new practice in your classroom, you have now entered the highway. Though your destination may not have changed, you are now traveling on unfamiliar roads and learning to use a new vehicle to get there. The turn signals are not where you are used to finding them, and the traffic is horrendous (or it is moving so fast that you can barely keep up!). You need a navigator at first to help you arrive with all passengers alive. It does indeed feel like survival the first few times out. It all feels awkward and new. You feel lucky to have arrived alive!

"The disposition for teaching is two percent inborn and ninety-eight percent reinvented every day of one's career."
—Susan Ohanian

This, our friends, is the point where the juncture for success or abandonment of changed practice will occur. It feels terrible to do things less than perfectly. That is why most people turn back from promising practice. It feels too much like failure, and we succumb to fear. Steve Barkley (2005), executive vice-president of Performance Learning Systems, describes this as an event that should be expected and is a natural part of changing and improving practice. When working with our principals and coaches in our district, he suggested that principals should look for one important piece of evidence to ensure that the coach was being accessed and used by teachers. The sure sign of evidence he shared is that the instructional delivery will look worse before it gets better. He reminded us that without an awkward period of adjustment, no real stretch occurs and there is no need to work with a coach. The easy change is done naturally by teachers and can be accomplished in solo fashion. It is the hard work of meaningful change to purposeful practice that can only be accomplished in the company of a trusted colleague—a coach.

Let's continue using the analogy of the student driver to get you thinking about coaching as a vehicle to assist you in reaching your desired destination. There is one tremendous understanding that needs to occur in order to move forward in your thinking and your practice of working in a coaching situation. You must understand that both the coach and the teacher are simultaneous learners and experts. You, the teacher, are in control of the learning experience. You get to decide when it is more helpful to be in the driver's seat and when you will receive greater benefit from the coach taking the wheel as you sit in the role of observer.

We will discuss the different models for working with a coach in a later chapter. For now, we hope you see that working with a coach is not about outside evaluation, but rather a thoughtful, reflective process that works from within. This process will guide you in pinpointing what is working well, and it will help you identify places in which you wish to see greater benefit for your students and yourself. We want you to embrace the real and true purpose of coaching, which is *not* to render judgment, but rather to seek information that will help you realize your vision and goals for your students. With this understanding established, we strongly believe coaching will be the vehicle employed by teachers who want to capitalize on the opportunity to make a difference for children. It is sacred ground we traverse. We invite you to use the questions at the end of the chapter as a guide for personal reflection or with trusted colleagues you have invited to travel with you as you begin your journey.

Communication and sharing lead to positive coaching experiences.

Let the research affirm you as a teacher. Let the message about the need for coaching revitalize your self-confidence as a teacher. You can now release all failed attempts and recognize there was nothing wrong with your students or your abilities. You were just missing an important and necessary element for making desired change happen—a coach.

Teachers Talk About Coaching Experiences

Read the following testimonials from teachers to learn more about their coaching experiences.

"Working with my coach really frustrated me at times. She kept wanting to explore what could be done with a few students in my classroom that I felt were beyond my ability to help. She was insistent. Though I walked away from her a few times feeling really frustrated, I am glad she persisted. We kept trying one thing after another and I finally did see improvement. Our screening and progress monitoring began to prove these children could make progress. I was finally convinced." (Amanda Madunic, First-Grade Teacher, West Tampa Elementary)

"Being new to the district, I was unfamiliar with the instructional models. I grabbed my coach and said, "You have got to help me." She helped me dig myself out when I got stuck. Making me talk it out helped me think it out. She helped by not giving me the answers but getting me to think it out. We ended up being great friends over time. It was the best situation I've been in during my teaching career—having that open relationship." (Emily Joseph, ESE Teacher)

"I had to have someone start with me at 'square one.' If I had not had my coach, I would have had no idea where to begin." (Sam Williams, Alternatively Certified Kindergarten Teacher)

"I had three coaches over time. At first I was afraid. Once I understood the purpose, I relaxed. The jitters left over time. With more contact, a relationship began to build through our conversations. We eventually became friends." (Cathy Tirpak, Third-Grade Teacher)

"The real difference was that my coaches didn't try to solve my problems but helped reveal the answers within me. Sometimes the lessons that failed were the ones we learned the most from together." (Jennifer McCrystal, Former Third-Grade Teacher Who Became a Reading Coach)

Reflection

Take a moment to respond to the testimonials of teachers who felt more than a bit skittish at the outset but who have moved to trust coaching and now embrace the work with their coaches as a necessary dimension of teaching.

Then, using thoughts you captured along the way, reflect on what has been shared about the purpose of coaching to complete the statement below:

I can grow and improve my instructional practice best in the company of others—especially a coach. The first step I will take is…

Taking the Road Less Traveled

Thoughts About Coaching

- Coaching is about personal courage, commitment, and confidence.
- Coaching is about asking questions and seeking solutions.
- Coaching is about taking risks.
- Coaching is about knowing when to take stock of your teaching.

Some Observations About Commitment

In a recent conversation with administrators concerning their role as instructional leaders, Dr. Grego, our assistant superintendent for curriculum and instruction, made a poignant point about what coaching asks of teachers. He asked us the difference between a chicken and a pig. He then proceeded to provide the answer. He said that the chicken merely makes a contribution to the breakfast table with the egg, while the pig makes a full commitment with the bacon. This anecdote provides a good starting point for embarking on the road less traveled and considering what coaching asks of you. As in all other quests, we find it takes more than a wishbone—it takes a real backbone of commitment to reach our goals through coaching. Perhaps this will be clearer in the story Mary shares.

Getting Physically Fit: Mary's Story

Many people come to a point where they desire to make changes to their physical appearance and overall health. This happened to me five years ago. Here is where my story comes in.

My husband and I are close friends with Phil, who has devoted his professional life to being a first-rate personal fitness trainer. Phil is an upbeat, energetic soul who is successful at his work because of the passion and high level of commitment he holds for it. He truly believes in helping people achieve higher levels of physical fitness and overall well-being. One day I was expressing my desire to become more physically fit to Phil. He graciously offered to help me after work each evening. Since he lived in the adjoining townhouse, many of the common obstacles were removed.

The first night we worked together, I was feeling pretty good. He chose just the right routine to nudge me forward in my exercises without too much discomfort. As days went on, he ramped it up and challenged me to reach a little further in my discomfort (as any good coach would do). Mornings came around, and I was starting to feel a real difference in my overall physical status. Though there was slight pain, the pain was a positive reminder of my active commitment to my goal. The payoff for that pain was beginning to emerge in small, incremental stages. I began to notice an increase in my energy level; my clothes were fitting better; my mind was clearer; and I was sleeping more soundly.

One day, I was driving home from an unusually stressful day at work. All I wanted to do was take off my shoes, put on my T-shirt and shorts, pour myself a nice cold beverage, and curl up on the couch with a good book. But then I remembered—Phil! I knew I had to make a plan. So when I drove into the neighborhood, I pulled the car into the garage, closed the garage door behind me, and quietly sneaked into the house. I proceeded to pull the window shades down and kept all the lights off in the house. I tiptoed very quietly to avoid giving away the fact that I was home. Then that noise came—the one that sent shivers down my spine. The doorbell rang once, twice, and a third time. A short moment of silence preceded that awful sound—the sound of a clasped fist pounding on the door. My heart was beating so fast I

thought, "I may as well go out to exercise with him."
But alas, I did not. I told myself I deserved this "down
time" to relax and unwind. Even Phil's incredible
dedication and persistence has its limits. The front door
became silent again.

Day after day I found one excuse after another for not
meeting Phil to exercise. He was always gracious and
understanding. He never sat in judgment of me or
made me feel bad for my decisions. He just said, "When
you are ready to make the commitment, I'll be here for
you."

Now as I reflect over this experience, I really understand
what it was asking of me. I now know if I want to make
an improvement, I must also make a commitment. I
have to find the fortitude it takes to break comfortable
habits. I have to be persistent enough to make the
changes part of my permanent routine.

In retrospect, I realize it wasn't that I didn't want
to work with Phil as my coach; I just wasn't willing
to drum up the commitment it took to render myself
open to coaching. I wasn't able to get past my levels of
discomfort. It works that way with teaching as well.
We have to be ready and willing to commit to our goals.
We have to be persistent in maintaining the commitment
to move beyond what merely feels comfortable to us in
the moment.

The Courage to Follow the Less-Traveled Road

"So, what will this thing called coaching ask of me?" you
ask. We can sum up the answer to this question with one
word—*courage*. Courage is a word we are certainly accustomed
to hearing and using. The word *courage* captures the quality of
being able to face your fears, the spirit of risk taking, and the
confidence to pursue the road less traveled. It takes great courage
to be committed.

Coaching does indeed demand courage—for both a teacher and a coach. It takes a good measure of fortitude to question our actions and ask how we might do it better. We also need to know where to focus our attention when starting to work with a coach. For teachers engaged in coaching, this courageous act of self-examination is an ongoing and rewarding process. Several coaching options that lead to self-reflection are presented in Appendix 2.1 (pp. 179–180).

A coach and teachers start working together.

It is this act of thoughtful consideration that helps form our personal theory for our teaching. But wait a minute! Didn't we leave theory behind in our college classrooms? We often think that, as teachers, we have moved into a strict mode of practice that is absent of theory. We may not realize that it is often our personal theory that forms our decisions and moves us to action every day. One definition of theory in the *Random House Unabridged Dictionary* (1997) is "a particular conception or view of something to be done or of the method of doing it." This definition supports the point we are making—your theory of teaching and learning shapes your actions in the classroom. Isaacs makes an additional observation about the role that theory plays: "A theory is a way of seeing…Without a theory, however—some way to assess what is happening—we shall be forever doomed to operate blindly, subject to chance" (1999, 73). We would never want to think we are operating blindly, leaving the results of our hard work to chance. We suggest that coaching can, in fact, keep your theory alive and working in a way that will help you accurately assess what is truly happening, as opposed to what you hope or think is happening. It will keep you from stumbling alone in the dark.

Let's look to our work together in this chapter as a vehicle that will bring you to a healthy theory for coaching—a theory that clearly identifies what you should expect of yourself, as well as what you should expect of your coach. You will need to be clear on these issues in order to achieve positive outcomes through coaching. Let's begin by revisiting some theory concerning teaching that we have already brought to light.

> *"Unless one has taught…it is hard to imagine the extent of the demands made on a teacher's attention."*
> —*Charles E. Silberman*

We have already addressed some operational theories that we believe most, if not all, teachers share. For instance, we have already observed that teachers work long, hard hours in their attempts to meet the goals for their students. We also agree that teachers need support in managing the awesome task of teaching. But here is where some might hit the first stumbling block. If you are already on overload, how can you possibly even think about moving in a new direction without any knowledge of what the demands will be? This is what we will try to help you with in this chapter. We will lay the groundwork for the courageous and thoughtful processes you will need to employ. This step is necessary to ensure that working with a coach will provide true and intentional benefits for you and your students. In other words, you will need to do some front-loading of thought that leads to belief and conviction (a theory) for what you expect from yourself and your coach. You need to define how you will commit to improved teaching through coaching. First, let's lay some more groundwork on the basic premise—the courage it takes to be coached.

Courage is trying something before you discount it: Find out, don't discount.

We have both personally experienced rejection by teachers before they even knew us or let us have a chance to explain what we had to offer. We constantly have to help coaches in our project pick themselves up and dust themselves off when they encounter similar experiences themselves. We find teachers often pose misguided reasons for politely (or not so politely) declining opportunities to work with a coach.

Just as we encourage our children to try new foods that may look or smell different, we find this a necessary role of the coach as well. Teachers are often reluctant to let go of current practices and routines to try something new and different. For many, working with a coach is the new and different activity they are afraid to try. For others, it may be that they previously encountered a less-than-positive experience and need to move beyond the bad taste it left. If you have not yet stepped into the realm of professional development via a coach, or you have stepped in and stepped back out, stop and think about why. This honest self-examination is the first call to courage for you.

Reflection

What observations do you have about coaching?

What experiences have shaped your thoughts about coaching?

What do you think you could do to establish an effective working relationship with a coach?

Once you have conducted the honest appraisal of what is holding you back, you will need to find the bravery to address it. You may need to approach your coach to help you move past your fear. We think this is the perfect place to let you in on a little secret: your coach experiences the same fears you do. Surprised? Just ask a coach. Most coaches we know fear that they will not live up to the expectations of teachers and administrators. Honest disclosure will be the first courageous step to take toward forging a trusting relationship with your coach and colleagues. As soon as we can let down our guards and find safety with one another, we will all be ready to grow. You will need to embrace and accept the fact that change will most likely make you feel worse before you recognize any improvement in your practice. In other words, you may need to admit you're scared of the process it takes to grow. At first, it may not feel good to change and grow. The old adage of "no pain, no gain" is true here, too! The main thing is that you realize and accept that it is your responsibility to grow as a teacher for the sake of your students. Take a moment to read the following reflection from one teacher: "It takes courage to let go of pride and parade in front of someone what may be less than perfect. I could always be selective about what I shared in conversation outside of my classroom. But when my coach comes into my classroom, that filter is removed." (Emily Joseph, ESE Teacher)

Courage is going public with your practice: Make your presence known.

This is all about the courage to go public with your thinking and teaching as you experience them in the here and now. It is about stepping out to share not only your strengths (what you feel comfortable doing in front of another), but being brave enough to identify and share places where you feel awkward and unpolished. It's about being honest about the places you feel most uncomfortable because it is not creating the results you want to see in your students. Stephanie Harvey and Anne Goudvis address the importance of teaching our students the power of making our thinking visible. They state, "When students engage in purposeful conversations and have opportunities to respond to their reading and make thinking visible, they articulate their learning and may change their thinking based on what they hear" (2005, 11). The same holds true for teachers. It is the act of taking your thinking to a visible process through coaching that can help you clearly see and assess your instructional practices. It is this focused view of your instructional processes that will help you revise your thinking and teaching. It is the catalyst for determining where you want to make changes in order to accomplish the goals you have for your students.

Courage is exploring ways to dive deeper and soar higher: Explore new directions.

Could it be that we often find ourselves operating only within safe parameters? After honest and careful examination, we may come to realize that we teach in a manner that does not expect more from us or our students than what we can comfortably deliver. Answer one question in this regard: do you see yourself as a pessimist or an optimist? The optimist invents the airplane. The pessimist invents the parachute (Stern 2006, 85). We would like to suggest that we need both the optimist and the pessimist operating together to optimize learning. Courage is the key to the balance we need in this equation in order to maintain the stretch of growth. We must possess optimism to soar to greater heights—where we believe and expect more of ourselves and our students (i.e., we need the airplane of the optimist). We combine the courage of stretch with the safety net of a coach to step in and cushion our landing (i.e., the parachute of the pessimist). We need to proceed not with reckless abandon but with deliberate thought for what we hope to accomplish in a manner that will recognize and measure both successes and failures. We will need to analyze both in order to determine what should be repeated, abandoned, or changed. We think we ask too much of you alone. Indeed, to accomplish this, you will need a coach!

Courage is toughing out the awkward beginning and mediocre middle to reach excellence at the end: Keep forging ahead.

It takes a good healthy measure of fortitude to outlast the initial awkwardness you experience when trying something new or embarking upon changing any habit, practice, or methodology. We can't rush the process. Rushing may only lead to frustration, which can lead to abandoning good efforts. We can't expect to move from our initial work with a coach to immediate and complete success. Steve Barkley shared the concept of the learning dip when working with coaches and school administrators in our school district. The learning dip is a concept that addresses the discomfort and confusion experienced when using a new skill. He explains that the learning actually suffers a little at first, but with coaching feedback, support, and celebration, the skill levels elevate to a higher level of understanding. You actually have to get worse to get better at something (2005, 45).

Of course, this is where we lose so many teachers in the process. Why would anyone want to engage in something that makes you get worse? Our answer is that the point where you dip down is only temporary. Soon you begin a steep climb back up. It is the same process we have in the field of medicine, yet we have no problem understanding it in that context. Doesn't the surgeon performing open-heart surgery make matters worse, and even pretty messy, before the patient experiences improvement? Think of it another way. Have you ever decided to tackle a really cluttered space like a closet, garage, or office? The first step to decluttering usually looks like you are moving in the *wrong* direction! To make improvement, you simply can't skip over the beginning and middle of the process to reach the end. You simply cannot avoid the unpleasant period and experience authentic growth.

Courage is stepping out beyond your strengths to address your needs: Take risks.

We pointed to the fact that coaching yourself to success is not only a courageous process but a thoughtful one as well. We bet there are certain parts of the instruction you deliver that you wish you could avoid. You may even find yourself sidestepping that particular area. However, when you move to a mind-set for coaching, this is exactly where it will take you! You will honestly identify what you want to improve. Your students will reap the benefit of your ability to teach with new confidence.

> *"Teachers should unmask themselves, admit into consciousness the idea that one does not need to know everything there is to know and one does not have to pretend to know everything there is to know."*
>
> —Esther P. Rothman

Courage is examining your routines and habits: Take stock of yourself.

This can be an easy area to choose for initial work with a coach. Just like chewing nails or cracking knuckles, we can identify teaching mannerisms that serve no good purpose and may even be wasting precious time and energy.

Don't be surprised if your coach also engages you in helping him or her break a habit he or she feel reduces their effectiveness as a coach. We, too, constantly ask for coaching as we work with teachers and coaches. Take a moment to think about a behavior that has become habitual and bothersome to you.

Can't think of one? Then here is the challenge for you! Videotape yourself teaching. You will no doubt find something you do that you will want to alter. It may be attending to only one side of the room, a verbal pattern of "Okays," or not calling on a student who consistently had his or her hand up during the lesson. Let us warn you, though—watching yourself on video can provide a wonderful mirror for examining places you can grow, but it takes a lot of courage to look. So take a deep breath before you take this leap.

Courage is creating a new image: Give yourself a makeover.

It can be a shock to the system when you make a drastic change in hairstyles. For men, it can be a huge step to grow a mustache or beard, or shave it off. If you have ever drastically changed your appearance, you can really embrace this example of courage. Each time you look in the mirror, you surprise yourself. You have reached the point of no return. It can be uncomfortable at first to see more of your face showing or having your ears exposed. Taking your teaching public with a coach can produce some of the same discomforts. It takes a little time to "grow into" your new style of teaching. We urge you to try it. Your coach will cheer you on, and soon you will be looking in the mirror, recognizing the new you and telling yourself, "You look mahvelous, dahling!"

Courage is taking on the BIG challenges: Confront twists and turns.

The issue of challenges is twofold. It has been our experience that we often create mountains out of molehills. Working in the company of a coach can help you tackle and tame those mountains you have created.

As for those mountains, well, a coach is what you need. A coach can help you find the best path to begin climbing that mountain. Once you get on the mountain, movement will be easier. Instead of standing back and seeing the entire mountain in all its intimidating enormity, you will start to simply focus on the first step you need to take, and then the next, and then the next. Soon you will be able to look back down the path you are climbing and see the progress you have made. And may we remind you how exhilarating the view from the top can be?

So what's holding you back? Strap your gear on, go find your coach guide, and start your climb to the top!

Reflection

Take a moment to identify a mountain that looms before you. Could this be a possible entry point for working with a coach? What path would you like to take for your climb to the top?

Below is an experience a teacher shared with us. In what ways does your experience compare?

"Running records was my mountain! It seemed so big and so tedious. I tried to just get through it for a long time. I just did them to meet a requirement. Once my coach helped me see their purpose and how I could use them, it all changed for me. When I began to take the record of reading with an outcome in mind, I attended to the task differently. I began using the information from the assessments and got better at seeing what was happening even while taking the running record. I think when something becomes meaningful, that is when it becomes manageable." (Jessica Ladoniczki, Former Fourth-Grade Teacher/Reading Coach)

Courage is standing alone in a crowd: Set an example.

Ever feel alone in your attempt to improve what you do? Ever feel like you stand out like a single blade of grass in a field of snow? Each of us has experienced the pain of trying to do things differently despite the protests of our colleagues. When you decide to enter a coaching experience, you may threaten the status quo of a school culture. You might actually find people trying to discourage you.

You will need the help of your coach to "keep on keeping on." Your coach will support you, cheer you on, and celebrate each step of progress you make! So go ahead—take that first courageous step and say yes to coaching. You will be on your way to a new and improved practice—practice that will benefit your students and in turn benefit you, the teacher.

Courage is knowing when to back up to move forward: Maintain your sense of direction.

If you have ever tried and failed, then guess what? You have just joined the human race. Each teacher is unique, as is each student and class he or she teaches. What works for one will not necessarily work for another. We often experience false starts that find us running off our course and into ditches. Do not despair. Remember, Thomas Edison held the belief that failure is essential to invention.

Reflection

Reach back to a time when something you tried failed. What did you learn from that experience? How have you carried that lesson forward?

Courage is daring to remain true to your dreams: Pursue that vision.

Do you remember the dreams you had as you prepared to become a teacher? Do you remember the excitement you felt when you took the keys to the door of your very first classroom? Visualize some faces of the students you have encountered where you know you made a difference.

Now think about how hard it has been to maintain the idealistic vision you had when you first walked into the classroom. Have you found that it keeps getting buried among the day-to-day demands that seem endless and often have so little to do with what you thought you were signing on to accomplish?

It's funny, but it actually takes courage to admit how discouraged we sometimes become. If you need to reclaim your dream, your coach is standing by with the cloth and polish you need to get it gleaming again. So come on—dare to dream!

Reflection

Describe a time when someone helped you reclaim a dream you thought was lost. What are some of the things they did that made that happen?

Find courage in the company of others: Share joys and woes.

If we have any need for working with a coach, sharing joys and woes with others sums it up. Don't you agree? It is scary to be a teacher and just as scary to be a coach. We hold sacred lives in our hands, and that is a big enough responsibility to frighten even the bravest of souls. We need each other if for no other reason than to provide the courage each of us needs to reclaim our profession for the best-of-best causes, our students, and indeed, our future. We hope you will have found the courage to claim the help that is available to you. Reach out to someone, a coach or other colleague, so that your reach can be extended through a newfound influence—an influence that will compound in interest and return dividends beyond compare.

Reflection

Take a few moments to read and ponder the following statements. Which will you choose to address by taking a courageous step?

If I am completely honest, I can admit that sometimes I fear…

If I could change one thing for my students, it would be…

If I could change one thing for myself, it would be…

If I try and fail, I know I can still…

Recognizing Detours and Dead Ends

3

Thoughts About Coaching

- Coaching is about taking control of your professional learning.
- Coaching is about a belief in the power of collaborative activities.
- Coaching is about exploration of beliefs and practices.
- Coaching is about observation of what actually happens in your classroom.

Some Observations About Misinterpreting Words

One of the mentors in our coaching project, Mellissa Alonso, shared this story with us.

"Miranda, my five-year-old daughter, went to the Cracker Barrel restaurant with my husband, Hector. The restaurant was featuring catfish that day. Miranda freaked out at the mention of catfish. Hector and I couldn't understand why she was upset. Later during the week, I was taking Miranda for dinner again and suggested we go to Cracker Barrel. She said, "No, I don't want to go." Now this is normally Miranda's favorite place, so I kept pushing her to reveal the problem. She put on a face of pure disgust and said, "I don't want to have to eat sea cat.""

Just as the word *catfish* caused Miranda's misconception, so it often is with coaching. There are a number of similar misunderstandings concerning the title *instructional coach* and the term *coaching* as they relate to teaching. We will explore the prevailing fears and mind-sets that often cause teachers to put on the brakes and stop what could be an effective vehicle for teacher growth and empowerment—their willingness to work with a coach. These misinterpretations have the potential to lead to detours, or even dead ends, in the pursuit of professional learning through coaching.

In the previous chapters, we have explored three important questions that teachers often consider before participating in coaching activities: "Why would I want to work with a coach?" "What's in it for me?" "What does coaching ask of me?" Of these questions, "Why would I want or need to work with a coach?" is one that perhaps needs closer consideration—it is the question that each teacher, administrator, and coach should ask before he or she begins working in a coaching situation. Yes, we include administrators and coaches in the term *working with a coach*. In an authentic culture of coaching, administrators, coaches, *and* teachers pursue coaching as an avenue of professional and personal growth. You, the teacher, as the end user, need to understand the power that *you* possess to build a collaborative and collegial culture at your school through your work with a coach.

Realizing your power of influence as a collaborative, collegial leader requires a full understanding of the concept of a coach. Who is this coach anyway? Is the coach friend or foe? To help you along in this process of understanding, it is important to take a few moments to explore your beliefs about coaching. The belief systems of the participants in a coaching program have the potential to make or break the power of coaching in a school or classroom setting. Katherine Casey observes, "Our beliefs about our literacy teaching are shaped not by what we read in professional texts or observe others do, but by the everyday interactions we have with children, every time we look for signs that they are learning because of our teaching" (2006, 191). This statement applies equally to all teaching. We have learned that beliefs can be challenged or supported by research, but it is our *experiences* that hold the power to *change* our beliefs. However, we also know it is hard for us to believe what we don't understand. A true understanding of the role of a coach is a necessary foundation for any reliable belief system to form about coaching.

Coaching Myths and Realities

Dr. Joyce Haines, who led our coaching project for a number of years, taught us the importance of recognizing myths and defining realities. She is correct in her belief that sometimes the best way to reach true understanding is to first dispel the misconceptions. In the following sections, we will explore myths that persist about coaching and demonstrate realities that characterize successful teacher-coach relationships.

Reflection

Take a moment to jot down what you know is holding you back from engaging in a coaching relationship.
In what ways do you think working with a coach could benefit you and your students?

Myth: The coach is the boss.
Reality: You, the teacher, are the boss—not the coach.

> *"Other people can't make you see with their eyes. At best they can only encourage you to use your own."*
>
> —*Aldous Leonard Huxley*

You are in control of your learning. You decide what your focus will be. You decide how and when your coaching will take place. You determine what the coaching session will entail. You choose the focus. You decide who will teach, who will observe, or if it will be a co-teach model. It is your responsibility to direct the path of learning you will take. Your coach will go where you lead.

Having all of this control certainly creates a safety net for risk taking, but it also underscores the level of responsibility you have for the coaching experience. With each blessing of freedom and choice comes a heightened level of personal accountability. With this freedom to choose comes the responsibility to accurately and honestly survey your own needs and then take the necessary steps to meet those needs. This is the responsibility you must accept and act on for the sake of the students you teach. But don't despair! Your coach can help expedite that process for you.

We often see a teacher's first experience with a coach focused at their comfort level, where they can share their strengths. This can provide a good introduction to the process of coaching and help build the confidence and trust needed to overcome vulnerabilities when sharing weaknesses. For your initial work with a coach, you may want to choose an area of competence where you can work comfortably at a level of refinement. On the other hand, you may choose to try something brand new, since there would not be any expectation that you would operate at any level of competence or expertise. However you choose to begin, do so with the expectation that you will receive feedback that may not always reflect what you hoped. But remember, this is the point of working with a coach. It is impossible to manage the many steps involved in teaching and at the same time capture the reality of what our instruction is actually accomplishing. Think of it this way: if it were so easy, we would not have so many teachers leaving the field so early in their careers feeling frustrated. In fact, were it not so complex and difficult to do alone, there would be no need for reading this book or for coaching. You should *expect* to need a coach. It's time to embrace the fact that our dear friend Regie Routman reminds us—"Teaching IS too tough to go it alone!" (2000, xlii)

We want to take a moment to praise you and applaud your efforts thus far. No matter where you may be on the continuum of coaching—you are on the right path. Keep moving forward to embrace this support that is available to you. Regardless of whether you have a person designated in the role of coach, we want you to see the relevance of relying on another set of eyes in order to reflect and refine. Once you take that first brave step with coaching, a glorious journey of personal reflection and professional growth has begun. Congratulations!

Reflection

If you don't have a person designated as an instructional coach at your school, think about whom you might form a collegial relationship with.

Myth: The coach is an evaluator.

Reality: The coach is a colleague who collaborates with you. Supervision and evaluation are not within the coach's role.

We know that merely telling you that the coach is not an evaluator is not likely to convince you otherwise. It will take a little bit of action on your part before you become completely convinced. Why? It's pretty simple, really. Think about the times you have had someone come to your classroom and stay long enough to see what you were actually doing. We bet for most of you, they were there to evaluate you. Although our administrators may conduct brief walk-through visits, they rarely have time in their busy schedules to linger and really absorb what is happening in our classrooms on a daily basis. Most teachers have never had the opportunity to experience in-depth observations of what they are doing that were not attached to evaluation.

We will suggest that, as with everything else, practice makes perfect. The only way to get over our jitters of being watched is to be watched again and again until we experience something new and different that stands outside the realm of evaluation. We are suggesting that it will take practice to bring you to a healthy mind-set for coaching. We challenge you to invite a colleague or coach to watch you multiple times and then, after each visit, hold conversations that *you* lead. We bet that after these trials you will feel differently about having a coach in your room with you. You will be evolving into the mind-set needed for an effective coaching experience. But don't take it from us. Read the words of a teacher who was most resistant to coaching but over time came to realize the power and value it held for her:

"My coach knew her presence wasn't wanted. I kept pushing her away. She persisted and let us get used to her. She wasn't pushy, and I was finally able to accept her. When I tried what she suggested and it worked with my kids, I was pleased with the effect. One success built onto another. I became more relaxed, and she became a comfort to me rather than a stress. Once I knew she wasn't running to the principal, I relaxed. Now I go looking for her." (Kara Sanford, First-Grade Teacher, Cleveland Elementary)

A classroom teacher in action with a coach nearby for support

Myth: The coach knows everything.

Reality: No one can claim to know everything about teaching and learning.

No, coaches don't know everything. We didn't know everything when we started as coaches and still don't as the trainers and leaders of coaches. Coaches are teachers and learners, too. They are your colleagues and co-learners. Their goals are the same as yours. Their goal is to grow the learners they teach and in turn grow from the learners they teach. They just operate a bit differently to accomplish these learning goals. If you can see coaches as you would interns working with you, your perspective will be much closer to the reality of who they are. They are learners who just happen to be learning in a multitude of classrooms alongside a diverse group of co-learners. For the coaches in our district, we can also say they have had the privilege of ongoing specialized training that most teachers (and sadly, many coaches) do not have the opportunity to receive. We hope you will approach the idea of coaching with the mind-set that the coach is here to serve you in a way that will help you better serve your students.

Reflection

Take a moment to track your thinking. Have you revised any preconceived notions from what you have read so far?

> *"I'm not a teacher; only a fellow traveler of whom you asked the way. I pointed ahead—ahead of myself as well as you."*
> —George Bernard Shaw

Myth: The coach is a perfect model.

Reality: No one can claim to be the perfect teacher—coaches, like anyone else, will exhibit imperfections.

Krissy Perkins, one of our dynamic coaches, uses the following quote as her closing in her email messages: "A coach is someone who will walk beside you to support you through the often painful, yet rewarding, process of change." Coaches truly embrace this observation. If you can internalize this message, you will soon be free of the apprehensions that often hold teachers back from being vulnerable enough to share their needs with their coach.

Although we both can recount numerous times our modeling was not all we wished it could be, join us as we share one particular example when one of our model lessons was *far* less than perfect.

Best Intentions Go Astray! Cheryl's Story

A school in our district was designated as a focus school because of low scores on the state accountability test. I was expected to provide direct support on a weekly basis. In working with primary teachers in this school, there was one teacher, Ms. Raucey, who begged support and for very good reason. She had the toughest class I had ever encountered. Ms. Raucey had been assigned to this class in December. Though Ms. Raucey did have some experiences working with challenging circumstances, nothing had quite prepared her for the situation she now faced. But she is a teacher who believed in her students. Her struggle was with her shaken confidence in her ability to perform at the high level of competence needed to move appropriately with this group of students. Control had to be wrestled away from the students, and the teacher had to become a powerful presence in the classroom so that students could feel safe and would be able to focus on the academic challenges they faced collectively and individually.

The reading coach had been dedicating a lot of time trying to help Ms. Raucey manage student behavior so that learning could occur. This brave teacher was more than willing to put her practice and ability on the line in the hope that through coached support she could move to a place of greater effectiveness when working with these students.

Our first visit was to observe her working with her students and pinpoint when behavior began to disintegrate. The agreed data was captured. Through our combined efforts to analyze where things broke down, it became apparent that students became unruly anytime there was not a strict code of procedures they should follow for an activity or task. We agreed that Ms. Raucey needed to back up and put basic procedures in place.

The reading coach agreed to take the class over for a day to allow Ms. Raucey to watch, with me at her side, and discuss what we were observing as the coach introduced, modeled, and practiced new procedures. Ms. Raucey observed her students interacting with the lesson, the coach, and each other. She began to note that some students were able to interact with certain individuals better than others. She also identified a few lethal combinations that she would make sure to avoid at all costs. Plans were tweaked, and it was agreed that I would take over the class the next day.

The next day arrived, and our plans continued to unfold positively. Even though some real tests of fortitude occurred throughout the morning, things were going quite well. Students remained engaged through the morning message, read-aloud, and word-work activities. It was now time for shared reading, when students would move to the carpet. Ms. Raucey had worked to set up a seating chart for the students based on her observations of behaviors the previous day. However, by this time, I had completely forgotten the sermon we had been relentlessly preaching to Ms. Raucey—the importance of establishing and following procedures. I called students back by tables in the normal fashion of procedure I used for moving students to the carpet. But this was not the procedure we had agreed would be effective for this class. Together we had determined that certain students would need to be separated in order for the class to function effectively. These students would need to be called individually and assigned to a specific seat on the carpet. My breach in following procedures was realized once the students were seated on the carpet. Students were not seated in the manner that we had agreed upon. Although the realization of some potential problems was immediate, I decided to continue with the lesson. I implored the students to agree that since they had chosen where they were sitting for the lesson, I was trusting and expecting them to behave in the manner expected. Ignoring the situation was not a problem at first, but as the lesson proceeded, things began to unravel. Imagine my horror when an actual fistfight broke out right in the middle of the lesson. The two students Ms. Raucey had determined to be the most volatile had in fact ended up next to each other. Her intuitions had proven to be accurate. I realized I had set myself up for disaster by not following our findings and subsequent plans. It was horrifying, humiliating, and everything else in between. Luckily no one was hurt, and the three of us were able to work together to restore order in short fashion. We continued with our plans. I worked with a small group while the coach monitored the independent activities of the other students. Ms. Raucey continued to observe her students and take notes.

It was soon time for lunch and our postconference. As you can imagine, my apologies were profuse. This most gracious teacher smiled her winning smile and shared that she had made up her mind that if everything had gone perfectly, she would have believed she was incapable of making the right things happen for her kids. She would have resigned in defeat.

Although this experience was most humbling, it worked to the benefit of all of us in powerful ways. It cemented the belief that we do learn much from our mistakes! We share this story with you to help you understand the sense of partnership found in a coaching experience. We want to dismiss the impression that perfection is the expectation at any level of the coaching experience. The reason for coaching is not to parade our perfections but to both realize and fulfill our need for continued growth as professionals. This story also illustrates the immediate serendipitous effect teachers experience in the process of coaching—that of seeing their students from a different vantage point as they interact with learning, with the teacher, and with each other.

Reflection

We have worked hard to convince you that perfection is not expected. What fears might you still be hanging on to at this point? Can you share them with your coach or a trusted colleague?

Myth: The coach works with the teachers who aren't doing a good job teaching.

Reality: The coach works with *all* teachers, providing support in areas that the teacher has identified.

You are not broken, so you don't need fixing, right? A lot of teachers have the attitude that coaches should work only with teachers who are failing and need fixing. Unfortunately, in some places, the way coaches are used supports this kind of thinking.

Becky Schryver, one of our reading coaches, reported an experience that illustrates why so many teachers have this misguided opinion about coaches and their purpose. Becky works at a school where there is a deep and thorough understanding by the administrators and teachers concerning the role of the coach. There is a well-communicated expectation that ALL teachers will work with the coach. This shared understanding envelops the coaching process at this school.

A new teacher from a neighboring county arrived at the school. The coach walked into this teacher's classroom with her calendar in hand. She planned to introduce herself and schedule a time to visit the classroom to begin familiarizing herself and lay a foundation for future work. The teacher almost went into hysterics. She began questioning the coach about why she was sent to work with her. She exclaimed that she had just arrived, and stated, "I have experience, and I don't need a coach."

The coach in this story has that wonderful quality of calm in the midst of the storm. She probed gently for more information from the teacher, all the while assuring her that at this school, it was expected that the coach would serve all teachers. As the teacher calmed down, she was able to share her coaching experiences from the district where she previously taught. In her last school, it was known to everyone that the purpose and role of their coach was to provide evaluative documentation for moving teachers out of the system.

It hurts us to know that an administration would assign the role of evaluator to a coach. We know it will take some time for this teacher to build trust in the coaching process. Because understanding about coaching is strong at this school, we know that this teacher can be healed of past misconceptions and will soon be on her way to coached success. She will no doubt be hurried along because she will have all three entities of the school staff communicating this to her. Collegial talk and sharing of coaching experiences is a common occurrence at this school, and the topic is threaded naturally in ongoing conversations. Eventually, she will be fine. Time and repetition of positive coaching experiences will help her overcome misgivings and begin to build a strong belief system in coaching.

We have many stories we can share about teachers and their fears. There were many instances when we first began our coaching project that revealed just how scary this prospect of coaching can be. One such teacher had not turned in a survey of interests for what she wanted to work on in the process of coaching. She came during conference night and, speaking in hushed tones, asked if she could have a moment of time. She began to explain why she had not turned in her survey. She was afraid to admit on paper that she wanted help in meeting individual student needs during guided reading sessions. She feared the administrator would see her request and lose faith in her as a teacher. Once she was assured that the administrator would not even *see* her request and the coaching session would remain confidential, she moved forward. This was a teacher who had always embraced coaching when she was approached by the coach to share something *new* with her. She felt safe when it wasn't something she believed she was expected to already know. But her desire to grow caused her to take a risk and let down her guard for an area she wanted to master. She shared later that the only thing that helped her move past her initial fear was her belief that with help she could learn new ways to better serve her students. She became a regular customer in *all* aspects of coaching once she understood that working with a coach and asking for help from a coach did not put her in a negative light with her administrator.

Reflection

Think about how you have seen coaches used. In what ways have these situations confused you? led you to question the value of coaching? led you to endorse coaching?

Myth: The coach will solve all your teaching problems.

Reality: The teacher is responsible for student learning; the coach can provide guidance and support in areas the teacher has identified.

Think of this little story we read recently in *Reader's Digest*.

Trouble was brewing at an auto company, so the boss posted this memo:

"We have not succeeded in solving all your problems. The solutions we have found have only raised a whole new set of problems. We are as confused as ever, but we believe we are confused on a higher level and about more important things" (Mullen 2006a, 88).

At the National Reading First Conference (July 2005, New Orleans), Mo Anderson shared that educators need to give up believing they will ever be rid of their problems. Instead, she suggested they should be about the business of creating better problems. Working with your coach will not solve all of your problems. However, it will help you identify which problems are the most critical to address and solve. However, once *that* problem is solved, we can almost guarantee there will be a another one rearing its ugly head. And, of course, you will want to address it. Over time and over multiple coaching experiences, you will begin to see your professional growth as an ongoing and never-ending cycle. However, we are equally convinced that at any point in your process, you will be able to look back at your progress. So go ahead and charge forward in identifying the first and most critical problem you face. Do this knowing that one of the most compelling components to teaching is that we will never complain of boredom because exciting new work constantly emerges when we stay in tune with ourselves and our students.

 ## Reflection

Go ahead and take a risk. List some thing(s) you know you would like to address to experience professional and personal growth.

Myth: A coach is there to make life easier only for the teacher.

Reality: The goal of coaching is to foster effective instruction that results in better lives for *everyone* in school.

Both a yes and no answer apply to this myth. You see, the goal of a coach is to make life better for the students. Coaches accomplish this goal through their work with the teachers. The work of a coach is focused on helping you, the teacher, examine how well your current practices are meeting the needs of your students. Through this process, you will be making decisions about what to abandon, what to change, and what to add to your teaching. Though the process may be tedious at times, the end result is well worth your effort. It is only when better things happen for your students that your life as a teacher truly improves.

Doesn't this make sense? However, we often see schools get off track in this regard. Many coaches find themselves operating in roles that do not directly impact instruction and thus do not improve student achievement. Coaches are often used primarily as test administrators, for school-level duties (lunchroom, hall monitors, and detention teachers), assistants to administrators, chief inventory clerks, and other random assignments.

We find there is a misconception among some people who think a coach should just be an extra set of hands that diminishes the workload of the adults in a school setting. Well, coaches *are* those extra sets of hands, but just as importantly, they are the extra pairs of ears and eyes. The hands of a coach should be used for holding up a mirror that has captured an accurate image of your classroom and perhaps the overall school culture. A coach's role is to help you see clearly what is *really* happening, as opposed to what you *think* is happening. Working with a coach will help pull the ideal practice you *want* to see and the real practice of what is actually happening closer together.

Okay, we realize this may be a bitter pill to swallow. Shouldn't working with a coach make things immediately easier for us? If you have been disillusioned or bewildered by the challenge and hard work that coaching requires, be comforted by the knowledge that you are not alone. You are hitting the bull's-eye target for professional growth. You want your workload to decrease? It can and will *over time* with the help of your coach. However, it takes hard work to change our habits and move from the comfortable and the familiar to new, more effective practices. But keep this in mind: it is only when you arrive at instructional practices that better serve your students that you will begin to experience a true, deep sense of ease as a teacher.

Before we move on, let's take some time to really tease out the purpose, goal, and subsequent result of working with a coach. Ponder this, please. If we make life better for our students, won't things be truly easier for us? Isn't that what we all really want? Did we not sign on to teaching so that we could have a positive impact on the lives of students? Isn't that why we are here in the first place? We believe it is. However, we both must confess that we often lose sight of this vision in the busyness and pressures of all we are expected to do.

Yes, the purpose of coaching is to make the lives of the students better. It is not always easy to do the right thing for students. Doing so often asks much of us. We quake and shy away from changing our practice because we simply do not know how we could possibly do one more thing. We are right to think this. Most teachers we have worked with have been working far beyond the work hours they are paid, and we mean *really* working a lot of *long* hours beyond their paid day. In *Good to Great*, Jim Collins speaks to this crucial issue when he writes, "The Good to Great people do not focus principally on what *to do* to become great, they focus equally on what *not* to do and what to *stop* doing" (2001, 11). So relax on one issue. The coach is not here to give you more to do. In fact, you may find that through the process of coaching, you will begin to focus more on letting go of those activities that are not serving a good purpose for your classroom.

Top 10+ Reasons to Work with a Coach

We hope we have provided greater clarity on what an instructional coach is by identifying common myths and the realities that counter those myths. Now let's revisit the compelling (and nagging) question again: why should I work with my coach?

We will make our suggestions, but we hope you will take some time to really wrestle with this notion so you come to own your ideals and reasons for purposeful work with a coach. To get you started, we offer our top reasons for working with a coach.

1. You need to have a keen sense of what is really happening as a result of your instruction. Working with a coach provides opportunities to step back and observe what is happening with your students as they interact with the teacher, the content, and each other.

2. You need support in gathering the very best materials for your instruction. A coach can help you sift through the resources to ensure that you are utilizing the best vehicles for your instruction.

3. You need help in reaching a deep knowledge about your students as learners. A coach can assist you in intersecting and analyzing data from multiple sources.

4. You find it hard to form a bridge between what you see in your ongoing assessments, what the results reveal about student achievement, and how to provide appropriate instruction. A coach can help you analyze current instruction and tease out the implications for future instruction. The old adage "two heads are better than one" was never more true. The coach can be a person you can feel safe to bounce off thoughts and ideas.

5. You need support in using what you know about your students to provide specific interventions that will target needs with precision and accelerate student progress. A coach can help you define the activities and select

resources that enable you to differentiate instruction to meet the diverse needs of your students.

6. You need to know what you do that maintains your students focus, as well as where they lose the focus you desire. A coach can help you capture this information so that you gain ground by increasing productive engagement and thus improve achievement.

7. You need to keep up with the latest research and practices to keep pace with our ever-changing world. A coach can model new strategies and techniques and provide you with professional resources describing these advances.

8. You need a shoulder and an ear. A coach can provide a comforting shoulder and an attentive ear as you sort out your thoughts and feelings.

9. You did not sign on for mediocrity. "Coaching provides a vehicle by which to achieve goals, improve strategies, and make a difference for students and colleagues" (Barkley 2005, 4). It moves teachers from good to great.

10. You are helping to mold the future of our world. Don't you deserve the kind of support that is traditionally available to entertainers and athletes?

And the most important reason of all, above all others on this list…You need to be in the company of others! This is because:

Our work as teachers is filled with dilemmas, with units we want to make better, and lessons that work great for the first period and bomb with period four. We want our assessments to tell us if the students have mastered the content. We want to understand how to help the silent voices at the back of the room. We have data, data, data, and we want to know how to use it in a meaningful way to drive the decisions we make in our planning and implementation of lessons that engage each student. These are the areas where we want to learn and grow. Who better to collaborate with us in managing and dealing with these issues than colleagues who share our context, our concerns, and our students? (Emm 2007, 30) So, really, we have 11 reasons to work with a coach. Hopefully some of these reasons will resonate with you.

To summarize, we offer this final thought: We engage in the coaching experience for the sake of our students and for the resulting peace of mind we experience when we know we are seeking to be the best we can be. If you are beginning to realize that coaching involves work—congratulations again! You have just discovered what it takes to be the teacher your students need you to be and the teacher you truly want to be. Teachers are not simply born, but rather develop the appropriate ideology and relationship skills by reflecting upon, learning from, and benefiting from their life experiences (Haberman 2005, 216). So celebrate the struggle. That is proof positive that you are an exemplary teacher who refuses to be satisfied with complacent mediocrity. You are the teacher every student deserves!

 ## Reflection

Now that you have finished reading this chapter, take some time to think about how you would complete the following statements:

I thought a coach was…

I now realize a coach is…

I think I would be okay working with a coach to…

I know I need a trusted colleague and friend to keep me…

Sharing the Driving

Thoughts About Coaching

- Coaching is about on-site, job-specific instructional support.
- Coaching is about strengthening professional relationships and interactions.
- Coaching is about becoming an objective observer of your own teaching.
- Coaching is learning to appreciate your strengths and acknowledging your limitations.

Some Observations About Relationships

The focus of our work in Chapter Four is twofold. We will explore various roles for school-based instructional coaches. Taking these roles into consideration will help you develop a working knowledge and sound definition for what a coach can be and do for you. We will address the relationship *you* decide to have with your coach and how *you* choose to tap the services of your coach. We want you to be aware that a plethora of options and a range of diverse choices exist for operating with your coach. You hold the key to unlocking this door. Once you have opened the door, you will share the responsibility with your coach for how your relationship evolves. By the end of this chapter, we hope that you will have a vision of how you can develop a productive relationship with your coach—a relationship in which you share the driving responsibilities.

Let's begin with an anecdote we found funny and effective in getting us moving in the right direction.

A mechanic accidentally swallowed some brake fluid and really liked the taste. Before he knew it, he had polished off a whole bottle of the stuff. His buddy George accidentally caught him sneaking a swig the next day. "That stuff is dangerous," George said. "You gotta give it up."

"Don't worry," the mechanic said, "I can stop anytime I want."

(Mullen 2006b, 88).

The mechanic was obviously way off in how he was using that brake fluid. When used properly, the fluid had a unique and important role to serve. However, when used in the manner described above, it posed grave danger. Just as illustrated here, it is possible for coaches to be engaged in purposes (although not as dangerous!) they were never intended to serve.

It is important to keep true to the purpose of coaching, which is to support teachers in improving instruction for the benefit of students. Just as the word *stop* has many nuances and shades of meaning, what it means to be coached can become distorted as well. We pointed out many ways this distortion can occur as a result of accepting the myths we identified in the previous chapter. Our first task is to help you think about the primary purpose for coaching. Once you have achieved this understanding, you are then ready to explore how you can reap the benefits of coaching. We want to help you stay true to the purpose of coaching and avoid any damage that might occur if the roles or the purpose are compromised.

Defining Roles of the School-Based Coach

The job of a school-based coach is a complex mix of teacher, resource provider, change agent, facilitator, mentor, and curriculum specialist—in general, this is someone who is able to provide just-in-time support to teachers individually or in small groups and help teachers restore confidence in themselves (Killion and Harrison 2005, 2005/2006; Richardson 2006). The primary purpose a coach strives to accomplish is to enable teachers to increase the quality and effectiveness of classroom instruction, which will lead to improvements in student achievement. The coach may achieve this purpose through a variety of activities, including conversations focused on instruction (Knight 2007a), modeling and demonstrating strategies, and co-teaching as well as observing and giving feedback on instruction or management (Killion and Harrison 2006d). Specifically, a coach has to be able to provide a range of services that are relevant to issues and situations that teachers have identified:

- assisting teachers with interpreting student achievement data to arrive at a better understanding of their students' strengths and weaknesses and plan instruction to address identified needs (Killion and Harrison 2005b)

- mentoring novice teachers to develop and refine their instructional skills as well as providing the moral support necessary to overcome the doubts so many of us experienced early in our careers (Killion and Harrison 2005c)

- increasing teachers' understanding of the curriculum by providing guidance in "developing pacing guides, preparing unit and lesson plans, developing assessments, and designing accommodations for various learners" (Killion and Harrison 2006a, 1–2)

- providing information about and access to additional instructional resources that facilitate teachers' efforts to differentiate instruction, as well as making available information from research that supports instructional practices (Killion and Harrison 2007)

In summary, Barkley (2005) notes that coaching for educators has a specific focus—improving teaching. Instructional coaches are full-time, on-site professional developers who function as learning facilitators to provide collaborative, job-embedded experiences (Knight 2007b; Killion and Harrison 2005). A good coach is an excellent teacher who is kindhearted, respectful, patient, compassionate, and honest. A good coach has high expectations and provides the affirmative and honest feedback that helps people realize those expectations. A good coach can see something in you that you didn't know was there and help you make that something special become a living part of you (Knight 2007b).

You will note that these descriptions of a coach's role do *not* include supervision and evaluation. Coaching is a partnership. "Partnership, at its core, is a deep belief that we are no more important than with whom we work, and that we should do everything we can to respect that equality" (Knight 2007b, 24). We want to make sure you are really grounded in this concept of coaching. Being clear on the partnership aspect of coaching is vital. It lays a critical foundation that supports your ability to embrace and use coaching for the benefit of you and your students.

Teachers and coaches have equal responsibility in this partnership process. Both coaches and teachers are in place to serve students. The teacher takes a much more direct path with the students, while the coach serves students by serving teachers. It is vital to have all parties on board with this understanding. Coaches must know and embrace the concept that the coach's responsibility to the students is realized through working with the teacher. Conversely, the teacher's responsibility to students is to work with the coach. Both the teacher and the coach must become conscious of the fact that "it's not about me." It is critical that we keep our eyes on the right target—the students. By keeping this target in focus, we will realize and embrace an overarching principle: coaching is not about the adults having things as *they like* them, but rather the children having things as *they need* them in order to grow to their optimum potential.

One of our coaches, Joani Altshuler, works in a high-needs school in West Tampa, Florida. She has done an amazingly effective job getting teachers to embrace the idea of coaching by putting the entire focus of her work on the students and how they respond to instruction. Everything that Joani does with her teachers is done with a focus on student data, lesson plans based on that data, and on the responses of the students, rather than the behavior of the teacher. This allows both people to have conversations about students rather than teachers and avoids making judgments or putting teachers on the defensive. Now, both coaches and teachers have a shared vision.

Reflection

In a series of articles for *Teachers Teaching Teachers (T3)*, Killion and Harrison have identified nine roles of the school-based coach. Think about each of these roles and how they might apply to you as you work with your coach: learning facilitator, interpreter of data, mentor, school leader, curriculum specialist, instructional specialist, catalyst for change, classroom supporter, and resource provider.

Building the Teacher-Coach Relationship

> *"The more deeply you understand other people, the more you appreciate them, the more reverent you will feel toward them. To touch the soul of another human being is to walk on sacred ground."*
>
> —Stephen Covey

As teachers, we come in contact with a wide range of human beings while traversing the path of our careers. The Covey quote reminds us that the key to success in any situation is the ability to connect with and understand the people (young or old) who surround us. This understanding is critical, especially when we aren't in complete alignment with each other's philosophy or thinking. There are many occasions when we come in contact with people who have thoughts and ideas different from our own. Often, with a small investment of time, we find that the viewpoint this person brings to us fills a gap we have in our own perspective. The key to gaining new and enriched knowledge or perspective from others is in how well we really listen. Alda says that real listening is a willingness to let the other person change you (2006, 85). However, there will be times when after really listening and truly hearing, we still don't agree. In these instances, we can agree to disagree with people, yet still find ways to foster ongoing regard for one another.

The key to working in a collaborative relationship with a colleague or coach is to accept the fact that your quality of interactions with each other will change depending on the topic or experience together. For example, when we first enter into a teacher/coach relationship, the conversation may be different than what it will become after spending time together and developing trust and rapport with one another. At first, both people may be guarded and very cautious about the words they use and what they share with each other. This is what we consider *limited-access language*. It has strict limits because we feel we have something to lose if we are not cautious in how we proceed. Even after a greater comfort level is established, a new or controversial topic may cause you both to revert back to this cautious relationship stage.

As you work and grow together, you will find that shared experiences help build a bond between you. You are still very conscious of the language you share and the vulnerability you feel with this person, but you now feel a sense of trust and ease in doing so. This stage is what we refer to as *varied-access language*. At this point, the language in the relationship can go either way. It can go to the cautious side of the continuum where conversation remains formal and guarded, or it can take on a more trusting quality of revealing our humanity to one another. How the interaction develops often depends on the topic.

Total-access language is the optimum stage of the relationship continuum and the targeted goal when working with a coaching colleague. A coach is the person who is willing to allow *total-access language* to occur as it relates to teaching. Not only would a coach allow it but they would also welcome it with open arms! *Total access* is the point you reach with a person when you feel completely safe in sharing your thoughts, opinions, celebrations, strengths, and even your weaknesses. This relationship stage is the ideal condition for true coaching to occur. At this stage, you feel assured that if things are revealed to one another (the good, the bad, and the ugly), it will be received with the utmost regard. Exciting things will be celebrated. Failed attempts will invite new strategies. Embarrassing moments will be kept confidential.

Figure 4.1, on page 80, is a graphic representation of these three aspects of language access. This continuum illustrates how relationships take on different characteristics depending on the topic or person. At times, we move back and forth across the continuum with different people. At other times, we move back and forth with just one individual.

Figure 4.1 Language Access Continuum

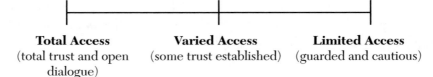

| **Total Access** | **Varied Access** | **Limited Access** |
| (total trust and open dialogue) | (some trust established) | (guarded and cautious) |

Reflection

Take a few moments to study the graphic. Now think about people with whom you have interacted in more than one place on the continuum.

How do these interactions differ in your professional and personal relationships?

What does it take for you to enjoy total-access language?

What causes you to move back to varied- or limited-access language?

You may be thinking to yourself right now that these stages apply to just about any human interaction in life, and you would be correct. We want to bring this understanding to your conscious level to put you at ease when you feel moments of discomfort in working with a colleague or a coach. We want you to understand that all of these stages are perfectly normal. These stages can be easily recognized in a relationship with a spouse or best friend when you engage in topics of politics, religion, sports, child rearing, or any subject that would cause you to move back and forth across the relationship/language continuum. Even though you have developed a strong trust in that other person, there may be a topic or two in which you will need to proceed with great caution.

Communication with My Spouse: Mary's Story

Here is a personal example of what we mean by moving across the language continuum even when you are involved in a total-access relationship. My husband, John, has made communication a top priority in our marriage. He is a therapeutic counselor by profession, so communication is an area in which he operates comfortably. For the most part, we can talk about the majority of topics without the worry of hurting or embarrassing each other. However, there are some topics that definitely require a "proceed with caution" sign. One topic that is very touchy for both of us is when past relationships are brought up in conversation. These are people with whom we were closely involved before we met each other. This is an area of limited access for both of us. Sometimes, the mere mention of that person's name creates an atmosphere of extreme discomfort. So we must tread carefully when the "ex" topic is ever alluded to or mentioned.

There are other conversations between us that allow for more open dialogue, yet full disclosure of feelings and emotions remain guarded. We often move to the middle of the continuum on these occasions. For instance, our varied-access language comes into play when we have discussions about finances and money. There is a need to be open and honest, yes, but there is also a need to be cautious or we find ourselves back at limited access with one another. We have learned to really listen to each other before we share a response that contains our own perspective on money and spending.

One of the most liberating aspects of partaking in a total-access conversation with someone you trust is the ability to share what you honestly think and feel. One of the topics that John and I can share total-access language with is the topic of our extended families. Like most people, we come from families that are formed from a conundrum of the complex dynamics of love, emotionality, distance, and physical ailments of aging loved ones. We almost have an unspoken understanding of our relationships with these precious souls who have the ability to impact our lives tremendously for better or worse. We can share whatever thoughts we have with each other on this topic.

How does this description of Mary and John's communication relate to coaching? Hopefully, you will be able to forge a *total-access* relationship with either a coach or a colleague where trust and open dialogue can be the keystone from which you operate with each other. If you are fortunate enough to have this person in your professional life, understand that there will be different access points from which your conversations can take place. Again, the topic will most likely determine your access points.

> *"Things do not change; we change."*
> *—Henry David Thoreau*

Before we move on, let's explore another example of what we mean by the influence of a topic. Typically, most folks feel safe in discussing certain topics—the weather, for example. Here there is no risk involved. Those engaged in conversation are sharing the same experience, but no one has any responsibility for the experience. This would provide an opportunity for *total-access language*. Here people can readily accept a variety of perspectives. They are okay with the fact that "some like it hot and some like it cold." Since there is nothing personally at stake or personally threatening, differing opinions are easily considered as just that—opinions. However, try walking into a faculty lounge at lunch expounding on a new instructional strategy or sharing a professional book that brought you to a new level of teaching! We bet the reception would be quite different than if you just announced a weather bulletin!

What we have shared so far is how our coaching relationships can evolve over time. How we choose to engage in conversations will express the place in which we desire to operate at any given time or on any given topic. We have also noted that with ongoing interactions and experiences, we will be able to move toward total access with our coach, which means taking greater risks and experiencing more accelerated growth.

Coaches and teachers working collaboratively to plan a lesson

No matter what the entry point may be with your coach, the idea of a partnership should exemplify the relationship you strive to achieve. When you can truly partner, you will find the most meaningful work can occur—work that will make a difference for your students and for you. To achieve this level of partnership, you will need to develop a shared understanding that each person brings certain strengths, knowledge, and unique experiences to the coaching relationship. This understanding will help both partners grow and evolve as teachers, leaders, and communicators. As Fullan observes, "The single factor common to successful change is that relationships improve. If relationships improve, things get better. If relationships remain the same or get worse, ground is lost" (2002, 19).

Reflection

Think about how you can develop the coaching relationship so that you know your responsibility to your students is being upheld in a healthy way. Consider questions such as these:

How well can I engage in honest disclosure about my teaching practices and skills with a colleague/coach?

Am I willing to speak up and share my thinking with my colleague/coach?

How will I overcome the difficulty of scheduling time to meet with my coach/colleague?

Working with a Coach

As we have noted previously in this chapter, coaches are expected to wear many hats in their day-to-day interactions with colleagues, supervisors, and parents. As on-site staff developers, coaches have a multifaceted role. They must read and understand the latest research in the world of educational reform and accountability. In many districts, they attend ongoing training with fellow coaches and stay in close touch with what is happening districtwide, statewide, and nationwide. They often belong to professional organizations that help them network and build their knowledge. These activities keep them constantly updated and informed concerning the latest research and work of world-renowned experts. Having all of this professional knowledge and training background equips them to respond to a multitude of tasks that teachers may ask of them.

In Service to You, the Teacher

One of the first things your coach should do is let you know he or she is there to serve you. He or she can be that second set of eyes, ears, and hands in the classroom. Perhaps you need just the right text or teaching resource book to nail down a teaching point. Maybe you are curious about a professional book that addresses a new teaching strategy you want to learn or refine. Your coach is there for you—to find just the right teaching resources to help make your teaching function in a way that best suits the needs of you and your students. Most of the time, your coach will know just where to get that information for you. If your coach doesn't, he or she will likely move heaven and earth to find it!

In our work with teachers, we have found that having a plan for coaching activities is really helpful—for both the teacher and the coach. Take a look at the sample coaching plan, Appendix 4.1 (p. 181), and think about how you can adapt it for your purposes. Preparing the classroom for the coach's visit is another important part of planning that will lead to success in working with a coach. We share some ideas for this planning in Appendix 4.2 (p. 182).

Assessments Reveal What You Need to Know

One way we can all work smarter is to use assessments to pinpoint exactly what we need to be teaching. In the age of accountability, we hear about assessments everywhere we go. Many times, a negative mind-set is evident when conversations arise around certain kinds of tests. However, assessments can truly empower teaching if they are approached wisely. They can reveal the point at which we should initiate our teaching. They can help us plot a course for differentiated instruction. There are many standardized forms of tests with which all educators are very familiar. In addition, there are diagnostic assessment tools and formative assessment strategies that help you learn more about your students' performance. Your coach can share information about such assessments and model the administration of these with your students. In many schools, the coach will present a workshop on administration of these assessments. Data dialogues are other activities in which a coach "facilitates interaction about what types of data are being examined, what the data means, and what the next steps are by asking probing questions to guide data analysis" (Killion and Harrison 2005, 1). Such presentations can be catalysts for conversations among colleagues to explore the value of these assessments.

Making Assessments Really "Cook" for You

Please understand that once you and your coach have delved into the administration of assessments, you have only taken the first step together. Compare this situation to cooking. When you have assessed your students, you have merely gathered your ingredients. Now you must carefully measure, sift, and weigh before you mix everything together to teach. You will need to take time to talk with your coach and interpret the information the assessments reveal. Talking about assessment findings is a vital next step to ensure that you successfully plan your recipe for instruction. Once you have the assessments laid out in front of you and have analyzed the information revealed, you are finally ready to cook. Planning instruction together is the perfect place to experience a partnership relationship with your coach. Both you and your coach will be able to determine if you planned the right recipe for success. You will see evidence of your success in what occurs with your students. Indeed, it will leave a good taste in your mouth. It will leave you feeling satisfied because you know you reached out to meet the needs of your students with deliberate precision.

Reaching Beyond Current Practice

You may want to take a lesson to the next level or try something that you have never tried before in your teaching. This situation provides an occasion when you can invite your coach to model a certain technique, strategy, or skill with your students. Perhaps you would just like to see how somebody else approaches a certain teaching model, or you would like to see how your students learn from a different perspective. No matter what the reason, a coach can co-plan a lesson with you and model that lesson *for* you with *your* students. After the lesson, you will talk about what each of you observed as the lesson unfolded.

By the way, it doesn't mean that the coach is the expert or perfect model just because he or she models in your classroom. In fact, in some cases, the model lesson may fail miserably for one reason or another. This should not be seen as a failure, but rather as an opportunity to talk about the realities of teaching and what needs to be done next time to achieve success. It is in this state of reflection that great ideas are born!

The Power of Modeling

Modeling in classrooms can take on different characteristics. Some teachers want a coach to model a specific strategy to students in a short, concise mini-lesson. Others want to see a larger chunk of instruction. For example, we use Reader's Workshop in our district to teach balanced literacy. A teacher may want to see a specific strategy used in the shared-reading portion of the workshop. On another day, the teacher might want to see the strategy modeled throughout all components of the workshop. It is up to you, the teacher, to decide whether you want to see something very specific or the big picture. You decide what is most useful for your own professional learning. We encourage you to find a way to focus on specific elements you believe hold the greatest challenge and/or promise for you as you watch a model lesson. Collecting data and observations about what you see can help you elaborate on thoughts, ideas, and questions in your discussion that follows the lesson. It is in the discussions that occur both before and after a work session with your coach when you will realize the real power for making desired changes that will positively impact you and your students.

The Co-Teach Model

When coaching was somewhat new in our district, many people were uncomfortable moving from watching a model lesson being taught to being observed as *they* taught a lesson. One of the ways many of our coaches helped break down some of that anxiety was by inviting the classroom teacher into a co-teach model. This allowed both teachers to equally share the responsibility of planning, gathering materials, and teaching the students. The teacher and coach would negotiate in advance who would teach which parts of the lesson. As time went on and the trust level grew between these colleagues, they would dialogue back and forth throughout the lesson and learn to gracefully step in and out to support one another. This collaboration often paved the way for the next step. This next step requires the highest level of trust and rapport between the two professionals in order to be successful.

Different Paths for Different People

> *"Genuine learning always involves dialogue and encounter."*
>
> —Clark E. Moustakas

It's hard to believe that we have done this much talking about coaching so far and are only now ready to talk explicitly about how it should look and sound when you are actually coached. We have experienced that most people do need to move through all the previous levels before reaching the pinnacle of coaching—the activity of one colleague watching another colleague for an agreed-upon purpose. To fulfill the desire to move and improve beyond one's present level of ability, practice, and understanding requires a targeted focus. Successful coaching involves agreement between two people to focus on a particular aspect of teaching. When coaching reaches its most effective levels, the words used between the coach and colleague sound much more conversational. It is a true dialogue between professionals. New, less experienced coaches often take on an "interview flavor" when starting out in their new role and trying to refine their content knowledge as well as their conferencing skills. You might hear many questions and different forms of paraphrasing. This means the coach is still trying to balance his or her focus on what you are saying with how he or she is responding back to you. Coaches are very conscious of what they are saying because they are probably operating in that *limited-access* mode of language. We implore you to be patient. These conversational skills come more naturally and quickly for some than they do for others. Please keep in mind that the last thing your coach wants to do is leave you with the impression that they are rushing to judgment or evaluating you in any way. Like you, coaches can share stories, laugh, empathize, offer positive comments, discuss personal issues, and listen with great care (Knight 2007a, 3).

Some people bravely want coaching right away. They don't wait to build trust and rapport. Those are your bottom-line kind of people. Usually they are more experienced and confident in their view of themselves as teachers. As much as anyone else, coaches need to build their own skills, so spending time with masterful teachers is a necessary growth experience for them. Typically, we have found that the more truly effective teachers are, the more readily they embrace the concept of coaching.

Think about your own experiences or your children's experiences growing up and participating in team sports. You will probably recall that the coaches spent much more time developing the more talented performers. Of course, they coached everyone on the team, but the shining stars were the ones that got most of their attention. Looking back, isn't it obvious that the more advanced a player was in performance, the more important the refinement of each and every movement became? The less experienced players still got the coach's attention, but the coach's work in fine-tuning stronger athletes made a much bigger impact on the overall game.

Are we saying that coaches should only work with our strongest and most effective teachers? Absolutely not! What we do want people to understand is that if coaches spend more time building talent with the strongest teachers, they are actually building capacity at school sites. They are growing and expanding their own expertise by working with master teachers. What they learn from these experiences can now be spread to all teachers in the building.

We think the concept of "less is more" is absolutely fitting here. A coach cannot be in all classrooms during a week and be effective.

Trying to cover all classrooms will result in "a spit, a lick, and a promise" type of practice. We all know from experience how ineffective this mode of operating can be. Nothing really lasting happens, and that promise made is most often never realized. A coach can be much more effective when focusing on fewer classrooms each week and actually building capacity with those teachers before moving on. The goal would then be to have these teachers build coaching relationships with colleagues so that even in the absence of the designated coach, ongoing professional growth can still occur. Thus, a coaching culture is born.

Reflection

Think about an area in which you are ready to be coached. Who will you ask to coach you? What is your target for focus? Why?

Looking in the Mirror

One of the hardest things to do as a professional is to take a good look at ourselves and be able to pinpoint our strengths and weaknesses. All too often the weaknesses come blasting out at us whenever we take a moment to self-analyze. We are often our own worst critics. However, in coaching, we have someone else's eyes, ears, and (hopefully) less judgmental perspective on our teaching. During observations of your teaching, an effective coach spends a larger portion of the time recognizing your strengths and noting ways to build and expand on them.

Sometimes, having a coach capture all of the powerful (and not-so-powerful) moments of teaching on paper is an effective route to take when we ask to be coached. However, we have found that capturing the lesson on video for a coaching conference can sometimes be even more valuable. A video allows both of you to reflect simultaneously on the experience. It brings added flexibility to the discussion by allowing you to pause in places where you might want to talk about a specific student or teaching point. The video eliminates discussion about instruction in the abstract—you can actually point to examples as you view and discuss. You will find suggestions for observing and analyzing videotapes in Appendix 4.3 (pp. 183–184).

Learning About Myself: Mary Shares

When my reading coach sat down with me to watch a video of my guided-reading lesson, I had no idea that I was having such rich conversations with my students about their books. She pointed that out to me. I never thought I was that proficient in that area. (My own worst critic!) She also led me to notice that I was applying high-level questioning without even being conscious of it. However, I learned that I needed to hand the control (the talk) over to my students so that they could learn to initiate the questioning and discussion process with each other. It was really evident from the video that the students needed to have a bigger part in that lesson. Clues came out in the video that prompted my coach to ask me some key questions that brought me to that realization. This experience changed my approach to teaching from that day forward.

Putting ourselves on video is a courageous step toward self-reflection and refinement of what we do each day. If you are saying to yourself, "no way," we completely understand! It takes numerous repetitions of watching ourselves teaching on video to get past the superficial discomfort of worrying about what our hair, clothes, or overall physical features portray on video. Once you get down to the heart of what to watch for in a video, it can open up a whole new world of learning *from yourself*. If you are not ready for that much self-analysis, we have found audio recording to be extremely helpful in a similar way. It allows you to just focus on your voice, word choice, and the kinds of interactions that you have with your students. You and your coach can create a checklist together of what is most important for you to listen for on your recording. This allows you to stay focused on what is most critical for you to learn from your teaching right now. A checklist for analyzing audio recordings is provided in Appendix 4.4 (pp. 185–186).

Advocate for All

We have touched on the importance of relationships among colleagues. We have conveyed that without trust and rapport, we cannot function well as a profession. The same holds true for our relationships with students. There are students whom we hold near and dear to our hearts, wishing that we could wave a magic wand and have more students just like them filling up our classroom. Then there are the ones that send us home to our families puzzled and perplexed. By the end of the year, our spouses know their names and ask about them with a tender smile and a wink. No matter which kind of student we have in our classroom, we are advocates for them all. A coach can help us see past some of the biases we may carry with us. We like to think that we can easily rise above our human weaknesses. But in most cases, we usually need a helping hand to get there. Just having an objective person standing by our side can help us get past the obstacles that keep us from being true advocates for all students.

At this point, we would be remiss if we did not mention one of the most essential partners in the entire educational process—the parents. Without the partnership of parents, our students' fullest potential will never be reached. Parents are a vital component in our equation for success. We rarely meet parents who do not care about the well-being of their child. Parents are often eager to know what they can do to help their child achieve success. The truth is, some parents don't know how to support the learning at home. Others know some concepts, but with more clear communication and partnerships with the school, they could more effectively reinforce the efforts of our work. We all need to find ways to be stronger advocates for parents. After all, they have the most important job on earth!

A coach can gather information and put it into a format that busy parents can realistically embrace. We know of many coaches who hold evening sessions for parents and families. They work in partnership with school leaders and teachers to educate parents on how to implement effective learning strategies at home. Many also serve as partners with teachers in parent-teacher conferences to help explain certain assessment results or give recommendations alongside the classroom teacher for a supportive home-learning environment. In essence, a coach works in a humble servant role to be an advocate for anyone who has dedicated his or her life to helping children become lifelong learners.

Reflection

How has your perception of coaching been confirmed or changed after reading this chapter?

What benefits do you see for yourself in eliciting the services of a coach?

How do you currently use assessments to reflect on your approach to teaching?

Where would you begin the conversation tomorrow if you had the opportunity to work with a coach?

Finding Rewards in Twists and Turns

5

Thoughts About Coaching

- Coaching is about embracing change.
- Coaching is about unmasking yourself.
- Coaching is about continuous dialogue.
- Coaching is about remembering that once upon a time we were all beginning teachers.

Some Observations About Navigating the Unknown

You Can Always be Snoopy: Cheryl's Story

Picture this scene—My family is sitting down to dinner. As we prepare to eat, I notice my six-year-old son, Kyle, looking down with an intense look of frustration. When I asked him what was wrong, he burst into tears and blurted out, "I don't know what I want to be when I grow up!"

Apparently, a number of professionals had visited his first-grade class and shared information about their careers. The discussion that ensued among these young first graders revealed that all of his peers had firm plans in their minds for what they would pursue for their future careers. No amount of comforting from me calmed him down. Kyle was sure he was already behind in life in a manner that would prevent him from ever catching up to his peers. Throughout this tearful angst, my three-year-old son, Curt, watched and listened intensely—eyes big with wonder. As Kyle continued to lament his plight, Curt quietly reached over to pat his shoulder and said, "That's okay, Bubba. Don't cry! You can always be Snoopy like me!"

As you might guess, neither Curt nor Kyle became Snoopy (though Curt did a short stint as Chuck E. Cheese). However, it continues to be a fascinating experience to watch my three children as they seek their own paths in life. It has not been a straight route for any of them. It is so easy for me to see the path that lies ahead for my children even when they feel they are stumbling along in the dark. I know the possibilities are endless for them. However, I do have a grave understanding of the angst they experience about the unknown, as well as the steps they take that sometimes lead to dead ends. From my distant perspective, I can see the big picture that for the moment eludes them. I often find myself in the role of coach for them. I mostly listen and occasionally prompt them to look up, around, and beyond the obstacle blocking their view. I have also learned to hear and heed their prompts that remind me that I must follow their lead for what their hearts and souls are calling them to do.

As parents, we must open our field of vision to embrace the fact that there may be multiple destinations for our children that are all good. We sometimes have to forsake what we think is best and support them in reaching their own callings of heart, soul, and mind. Or, we may need to adjust our lenses to recognize that there are many paths one may take to reach the same destination—one that realizes their talents, gifts, and skills at an optimal level for them. It's not always easy to be a parent and allow our children to grow up and away from our vision for them.

I share this story to frame our experience as teachers. We, too, see the path for our students and want to help them move along that path to a destination that will realize their potential as unique individuals. We have the perspective our students often lack, which helps us see when they are taking detours that will delay or prevent them from reaching this destination. As teachers, we must open our field of vision to embrace the fact that there are a number of paths we will have to construct to ensure that each of our students reaches his or her unique destination—one that realizes his or her talents, gifts, and skills at the optimal level. There are many twists and turns we must help them navigate in order to accomplish this task.

But wait—isn't our journey also full of bends in the road, speed bumps, and obstacles that obscure our view? There are also deep ditches that act as sirens as we fight to keep our teaching moving along the straight and narrow path—a path that will reap the greatest benefit for our students. Our responsibility to our students can be daunting; it is far too demanding to expect that we can accomplish it alone! This is exactly why new teachers deserve a coach to help them navigate the brave new world of teaching. It is also why experienced teachers deserve that same support as they attempt to find better routes that yield greater rewards. Though we may be at different points in our journey, we can all commit to purposeful teaching that will lead to greater payoffs for our students, and thus ourselves.

It is through coached support that we can best look up, around, and beyond the obstacles that sometimes obscure our vision. Coaching is a support model that is customized to your unique needs and the individual path that you travel toward your desired destination—one that will optimize your talents, gifts, and skills so that you can provide the very best to your students.

Examining Coaching Over the Span of a Teaching Career

Let's revisit the "You can always be Snoopy" episode. Do you remember when you first knew you wanted to teach? For many people, this vision of changing the world one child at a time began early in life. For others, it evolved over time from a more circuitous route. No matter how we came to this profession, there are certain common experiences we all share from our first days, weeks, months, and years as a teacher. Most would agree that in our early experience we were operating from a place of innocence and naiveté kept alive by our endless enthusiasm.

Experience and Expertise: Cheryl's Story

A college professor provided a mantra that has remained true in all steps of my career. During my intern experience, she kept repeating to me that it takes three years of experience to get three years of expertise. She was trying to settle me down to realize that I was not going to do everything well at first. She also was trying to help me see that you can't know what you don't know. I was so impatient with myself. Aren't we all? And for good reason! We realize our angst reaches far beyond our own personal needs. When we consider the young lives we hold in our hands, it takes our breath away to realize that we are not perfect in our craft. It is for the sake of those young lives that we must drum up the courage to reach beyond ourselves. It is this purpose that calls us to coaching. No matter where you are in your teaching career—at the beginning, in the middle, or contemplating retirement—you can take advantage of what coaching offers.

In this chapter we are looking at coaching experiences across the span of a teaching career. We think these descriptions will meet your needs no matter where you are in the progression of teaching experience. You can choose how you wish to navigate here. We begin with universal actions in which all teachers engage during coaching. From there, we look at different stages of a teaching career, beginning with the perspective of new teachers (Getting Off to a Strong Start). We then move to a 5–10 year perspective (Five-Year Slump). From there we explore the experience of teachers who have 10+ years of experience (Smokin' Not Smoldering). We end with the experience of teachers nearing the end of their career (Fading or Going Out in a Blaze of Glory).

You may choose to explore only the section that pertains to you in the here and now. However, it is our hope that you will study all the sections. By proposing that you examine all the sections, we want to accomplish two goals. If you are relatively new to the teaching profession, we hope these materials will help lay out a path for continuously tapping the resource of coaching throughout your career. In various ways, coaching can bring great benefit to you at each step along your career path. For highly experienced teachers, we invite you to look back. We want to help you remember your early struggles. We would like to think you will become inspired to reach out to coach and mentor our new teachers. You have so much to offer. You can be a force in ending the syndrome of the private, isolated practice prevalent in so many schools. You can be a key that opens the door to collegial sharing and support. There are eager young souls both small and tall who can benefit from your expertise.

Before we move on, let's take a moment to look at Figure 5.1, Teacher Career Progression: Promises and Pitfalls. This diagram illustrates the stages we go through as teachers while traversing the path of our career. Each stage has both positive and negative aspects, but all play a role in shaping our beliefs and practices. We realize that these aspects are broad generalizations, but for the most part, the figure represents phases and attitudes that many of us have encountered.

Figure 5.1 Teacher Career Progression: Promises and Pitfalls

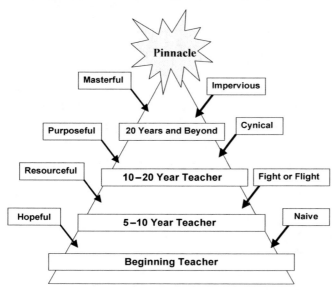

Reflection

Where are you in the teacher career progression?

What do you find promising at this stage of your career?

What pitfalls did you encounter (or are encountering) as a beginning teacher? How have these early experiences influenced you?

In what ways do you think coaching support applies at each stage in a teacher's career?

Coaching Experiences Common to All Teachers

Let's explore some universal principles for coaching that occur at all stages. No matter your level of experience, some factors will always be a part of what you do in order to realize the true benefit of coaching.

Who Serves Whom?

Both coach and teacher serve the students. You should expect to work together to focus on what your students need. An important benefit from coaching is the opportunity to work as partners. Working in the company of another is so much more effective than working in isolation. Having that second set of eyes and ears is priceless in aiding your ability to recognize who is actually being served by what you do. One important quest we should all pursue is ensuring that what we do actually serves our students in the ways we presume it does. By looking through a different lens, we often discern a reality that is markedly different from what we presumed was happening with and for our students. Whether it be watching as your coach interacts with your class or seeing the data your coach collects as a result of your work with your class, working with a coach can provide a reality check that will help you stay on a path that is serving your students in the manner you desire. Serving students is, after all, the mission of every teacher. You will be able to accomplish this mighty feat with greater clarity and confidence as you learn to hear and heed the prompts your students provide. Your coach can help you learn to recognize and respond appropriately to the cues from your students. The next step will be to identify the path you must take to follow your students' lead for what they demonstrate is their most critical need.

Dialogue is a critical aspect of coaching.

Talking Together

You will need to commit some time to organize your thoughts both before and after a coaching experience. No matter if you were watching your coach teach, co-teaching, co-planning, or asking your coach to observe you teach, the power of each experience will lie in the discussion that reveals your thinking about your teaching and the coaching experience. Talking together influences the next steps you take. Please do not think you can forgo this important part of the coaching experience. If you do, you are falling into the same pitfall we find with other types of staff development. Without time and an effective way to talk about and think through the learning experience, little change will occur that could make a difference for you or your students.

"Even the best professional development may fail to create meaningful and lasting changes in teaching and learning—unless teachers engage in ongoing professional dialogue to develop a reflective school community."

—*Regie Routman*

Data Collecting and Analyzing

Data gathering takes place before, during, and after a coaching activity. Without this important component, you cannot expect to hit an authentic target for your students. Which data you decide to study is up to you. It can be data related directly to your students or to you. Perhaps you have noticed that your students have difficulty making inferences. With the help of a coach, you could examine your instruction to determine strategies you could use to help students with this important comprehension task. Maybe you are reluctant to model writing for your students because deep down you don't consider yourself to be a writer. Or, perhaps you have observed some students who are hesitant to contribute to class discussions, but these same students converse readily and easily with classmates in other situations. In either situation, the data you collect through observation or assessment tools provides materials for discussion and planning with your coach. Your choices for data collection are practically endless. The important thing is that you look at data before the coaching occurs to identify where you want to focus your coaching activities. Once your focus is identified, you will decide what data will need to be collected during the coaching experience. After the coaching session has been completed, you will want to study and discuss the new data collected. Very often this discussion leads you to your next step, so a postconference can actually melt right into a preconference that sets up your next coaching experience.

Gradual Release Model of Coaching

We have learned over the years that coaching needs to follow the same model of learning we use for our students. Many educators employ the gradual release of responsibility model (Pearson and Gallagher 1983; Duke and Pearson 2004). With this model, we begin with a high level of support by modeling the task or strategy for our students. We then invite students to join us as we work together. Finally, we allow the students to try it under our watchful eyes before expecting them to apply the learning in independent practice. With coaching, we initially assumed that we could go immediately from modeling a lesson to having the teacher teach the lesson. In following this path, we met great resistance from the teachers. As we reflected on this issue, we discovered the resistance was most likely occurring because we left out an intermediary step in the process. We realized we had included the "I do" and "You do" portions of the gradual release model, but we needed to include the "We do" portion as well. We had long realized the value of using the gradual release model in teaching young students, but we now discovered this is an effective process for *all* learners—both young and old. To help teachers implement the gradual release model with their students and to demonstrate its application in coaching, we have used the lesson plan shown in Appendix 5.1 (p. 187).

Observing a Model

> "Society's greatest opportunity lies in
> tapping the human inclination towards
> collaboration."
>
> —Derek Bok

At each stage of your career, there will most likely be opportunities to grow by watching a colleague model a lesson, strategy, technique, or other activity. These activities represent the "I do" portion of the gradual release model. The situation may involve your coach demonstrating a problem-solving strategy for a group of your students, a colleague modeling writing with his or her own students, or a coach and colleague modeling a new classroom routine while you join a group of your peers in observing. It is always more powerful to watch in the company of a colleague—a conversational partner with whom you can share observations and thoughts. Often what one teacher notices will completely escape the attention of another. Watching a colleague in the company of a coach can be especially helpful. The coach will be able to point out details as they occur that will provide powerful topics for discussion that help in moving your thoughts and practice forward.

Although watching a model lesson is a powerful tool for the teacher observing, the one doing the modeling often receives as much or more benefit from the comments made by the observers. As teachers and coaches, we are often so immersed in the steps we take in delivering instruction that it is difficult to see all the other dynamics that make up the chemistry of a lesson. Just hearing what a colleague noticed about a lesson can bring to the conscious level many factors we may miss that can impact learning.

Co-Teaching and Co-Planning

Co-teaching and co-planning provide wonderful bridges that will ease you comfortably from the role of observer into that of model. Effective practices and powerful ideas will arise from the discussion that occurs as you and your coach work together to tease out the purpose, direction, and details of the lesson; who will do what; and what you expect to occur as a result of planning and teaching together. These activities are characteristic of the "we do" portion of the gradual release model.

Being Observed

The "you do" component of the gradual release model is one in which teachers often feel most reluctant to participate. We are aware that you may feel somewhat uncomfortable the first few times that your coach and other teachers observe you. Please remember what we have explored in previous chapters. Coaching is not about a performance of perfection. It is about professional growth. (Your coach does not do everything perfectly either. Remember Cheryl's story about best intentions going astray in Chapter Three.) Coaches simply have more experience in parading their teaching with all its imperfections for peers to observe, discuss, and grow from. As we mentioned earlier in the book, the only way to overcome the jitters that often accompany this aspect of coaching activities is practice, practice, practice!

Sharing

As you engage in various activities, you will most likely find things you will want to talk about and share with your coach and other colleagues. Our coaches and teachers find that team meetings or faculty meetings offer a good venue for a brief sharing of "ahas" and new discoveries. Email also offers a convenient venue for sharing ideas and findings. You may find yourself sharing wonderings, questions, and vulnerabilities in a variety of ways over time in your endeavor to accelerate your professional growth.

Go ahead and lead the charge on this one! We bet you can change the culture of an entire school just by conversations you start in the staff lunchroom, in the halls, and in those countless times you find yourself sitting with peers as you wait for events to begin.

Listening

We would be quite remiss if we went any further without speaking to the importance of listening. We are sure you have heard the adage that relates why we have two eyes and two ears but only one mouth. It is evidence of how much more our wisdom is impacted by what we allow ourselves to take in rather than what we send out. That's not to say there isn't great power in talking about our thinking—but we increase the power of our verbal communication when we add to it the act of thoughtful listening. As Marshall Goldsmith suggests, "Listening is a two-part maneuver. There's the part where we actually listen. And there's the part where we speak. Speaking establishes how we are perceived as a listener" (2007, 148).

Reflection

What opportunities are available for conversations about teaching with your colleagues? To what extent do you take advantage of these opportunities?

What do you think are the best aspects of these conversations? In what ways do you think these conversations could be made even better?

Getting Off to a Strong Start

Once we were both beginning teachers—new to the school, new to the classroom, new to the students, and new to unexpected challenges. As we look back on our first day in our classrooms, we both find that in one sense we remember it as if it were yesterday, but in quite another sense, it feels as if it happened to some other person we once knew. A lot has happened over the span of our teaching careers that has shaped and nudged us into the teachers and people we have now become. It has been a fantastic journey for us both. Looking back, we can agree that the old saying was never truer—"If only we knew then what we know now, how different things would have been." It all could have been different not only for us and the other teachers but also for countless students who filed through our doors each morning.

We remember arriving to work before the morning light broke and leaving after dark had descended. In spite of the early enthusiasm we enjoyed and employed, we were still operating in the dark in many ways. We remember feeling overwhelmed all the time. Each day we faced so many things that our college courses had not prepared us to tackle. In fact, most of what we encountered daily were tasks and situations our professors had not even mentioned.

If we had had access to the valuable resource of a coach, how many missteps could we have avoided? How many more could we have recognized as such? (We really *didn't* know what we didn't know.) Even more, how much could we have learned from those mistakes in the company of a coach?

So what does this mean to you? If you are a beginning teacher, allow yourself the luxury of having that second set of eyes, ears, and hands to guide you. Let your coach or a peer teacher help you step back to see the big picture. They can help you learn why some things work and why some don't. It is not unusual to abandon what could be strong, effective practice when all does not go perfectly. The guiding wisdom of an experienced colleague (a coach) can help you move beyond the obstacles, past the speed bumps, and out of the ditches. A coach can help you on your way to satisfying practice as evidenced in the performance of your students.

> *"Nobody starts out as a completely effective and creative teacher…The desire to teach and the ability to teach well are not the same thing. With the rarest of exceptions, one has to learn how to become a good teacher."*
>
> —*Herbert Kohl*

A Time and Place for Mentoring

There is often confusion surrounding support for new teachers. "Is it mentoring or coaching?" Though many call it coaching, what most new teachers receive really lies along the line of mentoring. This can come from someone who normally works as a coach, a peer teacher, or even an administrator. When a beginning teacher works with a mentor, it is expected that the mentor has acquired a level of expertise the teacher does not yet possess. With coaching, both coach and teacher are often working in partnership to learn a new strategy, explore a problem, or conduct action research. Mentors are often directed to work with teachers on predetermined areas of need, whereas coaching involves an agreed-upon focus chosen by the teacher.   Like coaching, mentoring requires ongoing communication about and modeling of effective practice. Importantly, the mentor must have the ability to convey optimism and hope in order to assure the new teacher that the trials and challenges of those first years in teaching are familiar territory (Rowley 1999).   Although many schools or districts provide mentoring support for beginning teachers, mentoring can often occur outside the formalities of district mandates. The informality of personally selected mentoring activities often provides the right amount of just-in-time support that you need as a beginning teacher. Perhaps you have a circle of "critical friends" with whom you get together regularly to share ideas about teaching (as well as other events in your life). The ideas you share in these sessions may well provide the moral support and motivation you need at a particular moment to continue in this wonderful profession.

Setting the Stage

Setting up the classroom environment is a wonderful starting place for a new teacher engaging the support of a coach. How you structure your classroom space will certainly impact how smoothly your classroom runs. The experienced eye of a coach can guide you in making wise decisions when arranging instructional areas, furniture, and designated spaces for activities in your classroom. Your coach can also help you establish important rules and procedures. This guidance provides a critical foundation that will enhance what you do in your classroom each day. You will find suggestions about how to get started with your coach in Appendix 5.2 (p. 188).

Assessments

In order to target your instruction to meet the needs of your specific class, you will need to become efficient in administering a variety of assessments, both formal and informal. Once the data from assessments is captured, the work of analyzing it begins so that it can guide your instruction. You want to make sure you are teaching the students, not just the lessons. Many a wonderfully executed lesson has been delivered with no learning occurring because of a poor match between the lesson and the needs of the students. Get your path laid out straight from the start by tapping the support available to you. Learn what to assess, how to assess it, and what to do with the results of the assessment. You will be miles ahead of the game if you master this component of instruction early on. This support will also assist you in reporting student progress to your administrators and parents.

Modeling

Asking your coach to model for you can save enormous time in teasing out how to put critical instructional components in place. Remember, a picture is worth a thousand words. Words can have so many shades of meaning. But actually seeing someone put those words into action can eliminate much floundering and confusion. But don't just take it from us. Here is firsthand evidence about working with a coach from a teacher who arrived in the classroom by way of our Alternative Certification Program (ACP): "The more I learned from watching my coach model lessons, the more I realized how much I didn't know. She helped me with the same topic over and over again so that I could learn it in depth." (Michael Coates, Kindergarten (ACP) Teacher at Mort)

Advocate for All

Don't forget that when you work with a coach, that person becomes very knowledgeable concerning your efforts to meet the needs of your students. The coach is acquainted with both you and your students. Don't ignore the powerful asset a coach can be in helping you prepare for parent conferences and also for presenting student concerns to child-study teams. Your first year in the classroom doesn't have to be a difficult and lonely time—your coach can provide advice and guidance when you need and want it.

So what will it take to grow through coaching as a new teacher? It comes back to courage—the courage to try coaching and allow it to move you forward even when it might feel scary to do so. It is the courage to go public with your thinking and teaching so you can ensure that what you do for your students is indeed what they need you to do.

Finding the Right Mentor: Mary's Story

Reflecting back on my days as a new teacher, I instinctively reached out to fellow teachers to get their insights and soak up their knowledge about getting through the natural learning process that every teacher experiences early in their career. I thought that anyone with more experience than me should know how to successfully navigate through the difficult times.

We did not have designated coaches back then, so we

relied on each other. Unfortunately, in my delicate, naive stage, I trusted any and all advice that came my way. I now know that you should be very selective in choosing the person who will coach your approach to teaching. Before I share this experience with you, I think it is necessary to give you some background information.

I moved to Tampa, Florida, to begin my teaching career. I came from a part of the country that was oversaturated with teachers and not enough positions to place most of them. My teaching internships took place in a very high socioeconomic area in Bucks County, Pennsylvania. The most severe behavior issue that I had encountered there was the occasional gum chewer or paper-plane-throwing incident.

Two weeks after I arrived in Florida, I began my teaching career. My first day on the job was at an inner-city school in Tampa and resulted in me collecting a Chinese star, a pocket knife, and breaking up a fight on the sidewalk at dismissal. These behaviors were all so new and foreign to me that I felt compelled to seek advice from a pair of seasoned veterans. They proceeded to tell me that I was just too nice and that I would have to toughen up to make it in teaching. So they graciously offered to coach me on how to survive in the urban setting. They demonstrated how to slam your fist onto a desk to get attention and control. They modeled the fine art of kicking a trash can without harming a student but gaining "respect." They spent many hours after school coaching me on the techniques of being a tough teacher. Needless to say, I smiled and nodded and showed my appreciation for their willingness to mentor me, but that was not how I wanted my classroom environment to operate. I quickly learned that intimidation and threats are definitely not the way you get students to learn and grow.

I knew that I had to seek out a mentor or coach who

shared my beliefs and philosophy. Then, like an answered prayer, she showed up on my doorstep. She was almost angelic in the way she interacted with both children and adults. She informed me that she was my PNE (Preparing New Educators) mentor. Before she had a chance to watch me in my classroom, she invited me into hers while my students went to music class. When I walked into her classroom, I felt like I was in somebody's house. The windows were draped with a pretty, sheer fabric. There were two big, fluffy couches in the back of the room for readers. There was a science station with collections of equipment, rocks, bugs, small animals, and plants that students were monitoring. The overhead florescent tube lights were turned off to reveal the soft lighting of various garage-sale lamps scattered around the room. The room just oozed with a student-centered environment. When she taught, her students were engaged and having dialogue with each other in a very respectful manner. That's when I knew I was forming a partnership with someone who shared many of my beliefs and could help me move forward in my career.

Previously, I had revealed my weaknesses to three colleagues in hopes that they would guide me in the right direction. However, I realize now how critical it is to be mentored or coached by the right kind of people, even when many offer to help with the best of intentions. As a new teacher, it may not be immediately clear to you who will be the person that will lead you down the right path. Just know that the right coach will always treat students with respect and be supportive in any situation.

Reflection

Use the quote that follows to start your own thinking about the direction you want to move with coaching.

> My perception of what a coach should do was...they should teach me how to teach. Now after working with her, I realize that that is only a part of it...What she *really* did was to teach me how to think about my own teaching. I never realized how many fundamental things I was leaving out of my teaching! (Michael Coates, Kindergarten (ACP) Teacher at Mort)

Who might I approach for coaching?

What would I hope to accomplish by working with this person?

Five-Year Slump

An Embarrassing Moment: Our Story About a Friend

This teacher/mentor/friend spent many years of her career as a fabulous kindergarten teacher. She shared this story with us that left us in tears laughing. She had just finished her annual Thanksgiving feast with her kindergarten class. She was dressed in pilgrim attire over her regular clothes. Knowing she would be more comfortable for the remainder of the day absent the pilgrim frock, she decided to quickly remove it before continuing on with the day's lessons. Imagine her horror when she peeled her pilgrim's dress off as well as her blouse underneath. With students' eyes and mouths wide open in surprise, she did the only thing she could think to do. She quickly jumped into her closet, reclothed herself, and tried to regain some professional composure before rejoining her class.

This type of "exposure" points perfectly to what we call the Wizard of Oz syndrome many of us experience. Remember the scene when Toto pulls back the curtain to reveal the wizard as a mere man? The wizard tries to dissuade people from the revelation of who he really is by repeated exclamations of "Pay no attention to the man behind the curtain!" So, what does this have to do with teachers? By the time we have spent a handful of years in teaching, we are seen as experienced experts—the wizards. It can be frightening to admit to ourselves that we still have burning questions and places we feel less than accomplished. We often find ourselves hiding behind a fabricated curtain or facade, afraid to be exposed as less than perfect in all we think, feel, and do. Both of us have experienced this phenomenon as teachers and coaches. As teachers, we had moved from not knowing what we did not know to becoming very aware of what we needed to know. We often found that what we now needed seemed elusive and out of reach. As coaches, our experience has been that many teachers in this phase offer great resistance to coaching. It is here that many teachers feel that their options are limited. Since we expect we should have learned all there is to know (or maybe we think this is what others expect of us), we may only see two options: fight or flight! We can fight our need for support. We might fight it because we are afraid to admit we need support. We might fight it because we are afraid it will ask more of us than we can possibly deliver. (See Chapter Two for a refresher on how real and common this fear is.) The only other option we see is to take flight from our chosen career, feeling a sense of failure. We feel we have failed because we did not reach our own expectations or what we presume others expected of us. Though you may not have actually taken either of these actions, most teachers we know have fought an ongoing mental battle with these haunting thoughts.

From what we have shared so far, it is obvious that this stage is often a critical juncture for teachers. They now have some experience that often has them functioning at a level that gets them through the day and even the year. However, at this stage, teachers often wonder, "Is this as good as it gets?" This fragile stage is when teachers, now perhaps more than ever, realize the enormity of the task before them. Idealism begins to fade to realism. Statistics show that approximately one-quarter of all beginning teachers leave the profession in the first five years, and those rates can climb to 50 percent in high-poverty areas (National Center for Education Statistics [NCES] 2007). Disenchantment, often fueled by lack of support, causes many disillusioned teachers to simply pack up and leave the profession. Others who stay may become discouraged by their lack of control over so many issues that impact and compound the difficulty of teaching. They feel alone and abandoned. Many now know what they don't know, but they are afraid to admit what they don't yet know. They often feel isolated and inadequate.

There are also plenty of folks at this stage who are well established in their pedagogy and ability to meet the challenges of the classroom. But they also run grave risks at this stage. They risk becoming stuck in a practice that eventually causes them to stagnate. Disenchantment and ho-hum boredom often plague these teachers. For all teachers at this stage, coaching can help to guide you to a new level of expertise and energy. Let's take a few moments to explore how this can work for all teachers when they reach this critical stage of their career.

You Take the Lead with Your Coach

It is important to remind you at this point that your coach is here to serve you. The questions all lie with you. Where do YOU see the need to grow and change to better meet the needs of your students? Now that you have "arrived alive," where will you go from here?

Might we suggest that a good place to begin is to inventory your routines in instruction and ask yourself why you do what you do each day? What do you expect is happening? Does this match what should be expected of your class as documented in your state standards or what you know about your students? As you ponder questions of this nature, you will probably land on one or two routines that may have become empty habits—things you do because they work to manage your class rather than positively affect your students' growth as learners. It may be that you do things because that was how you were taught by others.

Congratulations! You have now reached a peak in progress where you can begin to effectively question your own practice. It takes a measure of that courage we spoke of in Chapter Two to reflect honestly. Your coach can help you think through these ponderings. Use your coach as a sounding board to help you assess where you feel strong, where you feel concern, and where you wonder which of the two it is.

Reflection

Think back to Chapter Two and the descriptions of the kinds of courage needed to take the less-traveled road. What courageous steps do you think you need to take in order to expand on what you already know about your teaching?

Assessments

No matter where you are in the teacher career progression, you will never move beyond the need to use assessments. It is the information you derive from assessments that drives your instruction at every stage of your career. You use them to measure what your students have mastered, as well as what they need. You also use them to assess what you do well and pose questions for places you may not be hitting the appropriate target for your students. You now have the basic foundations of classroom management in place. You have a good working knowledge of the curriculum and supporting materials. The use of assessments is a powerful and efficient way to begin to direct the next steps of your professional growth.

Reflection

Which assessments provide clear guidance for what you do as a teacher?

How do you use them to ensure you are moving effectively with your instruction?

Where do you think you need to improve in your use of assessments?

Reaching Beyond Current Practice

> *"Occasionally…what you have to do is go back to the beginning and see everything in a new way."*
>
> —*Peter Straub*

Teachers at the 5–10 year phase have often adopted teaching practices that become routine and fixed. You may want to ask your coach to help you identify places where you may be operating within your comfort zone rather than working to meet the needs of your students. Combining the information you have from student assessments with the data you collect on your teaching routines will provide the basis for examining where you may be stuck in the rut of a routine. Don't despair—it happens to all of us. It is an easy trap to fall into given all the pressures and demands we face each day. We have found that a sure sign we had entered mindless-motion mode was when we did not have to think as we planned. This inattentiveness became a red flag that usually revealed we were slipping into teaching lessons, not students.

When trying out new practices to strengthen our instruction, we find that first we feel less than expert. It is sometimes hard to embrace the discomfort that comes with trying new things. Even as we gain experience with new practices, we find parts that do not produce the effect we desire or expect. Just like the new teacher, we often abandon what could be strong, effective practice when all does not go perfectly. We are sometimes too quick to abandon a new strategy or approach when actually some minor adjustments could have led to the results we wanted.

We know that change is not easy. If it were easy, you would have no need for peer or coach support. Ask a coach to help support you as you bravely look, examine, question, and work to improve what you do in your teaching practices. You will be on your way to ensuring you will become a teacher still on fire and smokin' as you reach the next stage of your path.

A Veteran Teacher's Coaching Story

Betty had been teaching for 12 years before a new coach had been assigned to her school. She heard from her teacher friends that the purpose of this coaching position was to spy on teachers and tell them what they were doing wrong. When the new coach popped into her classroom at the beginning of the year and introduced herself, Betty politely dismissed her by acting very focused on a name tag task and writing up next week's lesson plans. The new coach sensed Betty's discomfort. In an effort to establish trust and rapport, the coach left a small bundle of homemade cookies, a pencil, and a little note of introduction dangling from a ribbon that tied the small package together. Betty smiled, thanked her, and then resumed her work at her desk. "I don't need a coach. I have been teaching for 12 years. Your time would be better spent down the hallway with all those new teachers," she said with a polite smile.

The new coach got the message loud and clear. She knew that she would really have to work hard to build credibility and trust in order to get into Betty's classroom. Betty was not the only veteran teacher who thought that experienced teachers should not have to work with a coach. This was a widely accepted misconception about coaching across the district. Some administrators fostered this belief by only assigning coaches to new or struggling teachers. Because of this situation, Betty's friends were able to convince her that working with a coach meant there was something lacking in her teaching. Fortunately, for this new coach, *her* principal was very well read in the area of professional-development research and effective coaching practices.

At the next faculty meeting, the principal presented some snippets of research about coaching to the staff. He brought to light the fact that the more experienced you are in your career, the more you benefit from coaching. He showed many diagrams and examples that gave credence to the advantage of coaching in all stages of your teaching career. Betty listened with cynical ears but considered giving it a try anyway. When the meeting adjourned, she sought out the coach and asked her to come to her room and model a lesson for her. The coach was delighted, especially because three other people were standing behind Betty waiting to sign up for coaching services.

The next day, the new coach met with Betty to find out exactly what she needed to see in a model. They agreed upon the teaching point, and the coach came back during her reading block and modeled a lesson with Betty's class. After the lesson, they sat down together and talked about the things that Betty observed in the lesson. The two negotiated what should come next to narrow the focus. Betty asked the coach to watch her teach a similar lesson, observe the behaviors of the students, and record their responses to see if there was true understanding. The coach very objectively wrote down what the students did during the lesson and how they responded. Betty and the coach noticed characteristics in each other's teaching that would be useful for extending lesson activities in order to take students deeper into the learning.

Consequently, they decided to co-plan and co-teach the next lesson, videotape it, and watch it together. Since Betty had so much expertise and knowledge about teaching, the coach could take their conversations to a much higher level than what she had been doing with the new teachers down the hall. Betty realized that coaching at this level means refining your work and making yourself reach even higher in your teaching practice. She realized that coaching looks different in every classroom. Her teacher friends were wrong about coaches. Betty's coach never made her feel like she was doing something wrong; she just asked her to reflect and find her own ways of refining her teaching. Overall, the experience made Betty feel more empowered and less isolated in her classroom.

Reflection

What practices do you need to examine to ensure that they are serving, and not merely managing, your students?

What do you do to keep yourself motivated and enthusiastic about teaching?

In what ways does your teaching experience help create an effective working relationship with a coach?

Smokin' Not Smoldering

Dealing with Change: Our Story About Teachers' Reactions

What? No worksheets? This was the complaint we heard from teachers when our district first adopted a new core-reading program. In that first year of our adoption, we witnessed two very distinct responses from teachers. There were teachers who began to explore the new program with eager enthusiasm. They saw this new resource as a way to renew and strengthen their instruction. They worked in collaboration with colleagues to discern what would need to change and what must not change in order to use the materials effectively to meet students' needs. However, many other teachers resisted letting go of the old program and lamented the fact that there were different expectations for teaching with the new materials (like no worksheets). We began to see two different aspects of teacher behavior surface. While some teachers used the change as an opportunity to become better in their craft ("smokin'" was how we described this attitude), many others turned off and refused to change their teaching. Instead, they preferred to remain trapped in the familiar practices of old ("smoldering" was how we described this behavior).

So what does "smokin' not smoldering" mean? We have observed that as teachers move beyond five years of teaching, they tend to choose a path that leads to one of these destinations. They have arrived as full-blown teachers, having moved past those starting years and survived the five-year slump. Teachers at this stage usually hit a plateau in which the basic teaching skill is well within their control. They often reach a fork in their career path. They must decide if they are content to merely roll along maintaining the status quo or if they will find the courage to continue to grow beyond the basic skill set they have acquired. They must decide to move to smokin' or allow themselves to merely simmer down to what often leads to an experience of smoldering complacency.

The smokin' teachers are those who are ready to reflect and refine. They remain open to new ideas. They are ready for new challenges and eagerly take on leadership roles. These teachers are always urging themselves on in their quest to move from good to great. In fact, what they took to a level of great performance one year becomes their measure of merely good performance the following year. No matter what challenges they face, they always look within to find the measure it will take to continue to grow in their expertise and meet the needs of their students.

The smoldering teachers, by contrast, have not been able to find the resources to remain on the cutting edge. They experience a sense of burnout at this stage. They often revert to survival mode, clinging to routines that fall short of meeting student needs and merely get them through the day safely. Due to the daily pressures, lack of support systems, or a smoldering culture in the school where they teach, they find themselves exhausted. It is at this point when many teachers who could move to smokin' succumb to these negative factors and begin to smolder in complacent practice.

A couple of signs indicate that teachers may be headed down the path to smoldering. One is that they constantly feel that any action to improve or change causes them to feel like they are swimming upstream against the current. They may even feel pressure from peers to abandon efforts to change. Another danger signal is the feeling of hopelessness about the situation. Such feeling can lead teachers to begin to focus only on factors that are beyond their control, rather than empowering themselves to affect change where their influence will be felt. But of course, hope is available to all who find themselves fighting on this particular front. We suggest that you not walk but *run* to your coach! Share your frustrations. Share your concerns. Then get ready to roll up your sleeves and partner with your coach to move yourself toward brilliance and away from burnout. Let's explore some ways a coach can help you reach for new heights and depths as a seasoned teacher.

Advocate for All

We find many teachers at this stage feel they have no voice or power to impact their current culture, which may be inviting them to the smoldering side of the continuum. We believe teachers desire to work where they feel both inspired and empowered to continue down a path of positive professional growth. We suggest that all teachers truly desire to be on the smokin' side of this continuum. But as we said before, desire, though necessary, is not sufficient to make the change occur. It will take a real measure of courage to move that desire into real and effective action.

It is important to remember that you are not alone in this endeavor. Coaches continue to work as voices and vehicles for all teachers and students. Your coach can be your best asset for bringing about needed change for your individual needs or the collective needs of your team or school. Remember, it is the power of conversations that can change the world. "A good conversation is neither a fight nor a contest. Circular in form, cooperative in manner, and constructive in intent, it is an interchange of ideas by those who see themselves not as adversaries but as human beings come together to talk and listen and to learn from one another" (Martin 1985, 85). We just bet you are not alone in your desire to move forward. Your coach can be the first stop on an exciting journey as you step into a position of leadership with your peers.

Looking in the Mirror

As we stated in Chapter Four, one of the hardest things for professionals to do is to take a good look at ourselves and be able to pinpoint our strengths and weaknesses. At this stage in your career, much can be gained by looking to see where you have become autonomous in your practice. That is—look for things you don't even realize you do that are effective strategies and techniques. Remember that an effective coach spends a larger portion of the time observing your strengths and noting ways to build and expand on them. You need to do that too. We hope you will employ your coach to not only do direct observations but also work with you to videotape and analyze lessons. Look for your strengths. You will not miss something you feel is weak, so no effort will be needed to accomplish that task. We, of course, embrace the process of identifying a weakness, but that is only part of coaching. It is when you analyze your strengths that you can serve two mighty purposes. One purpose is that you will quite likely find something there that will guide you to shore up a weak area. The other purpose is that you become conscious of your talents and skills so that you can share them with others. Though this may sound obvious, often it is not at all!

Knowing What You Know: Cheryl's Story

I remember working with my dear friend and colleague Ellen Oberschall. She was a mentor and coach to me at a time when I had no designated coach to work with. Ellen is one of those teachers who is never satisfied with her current performance in her classroom, but always striving to grow and refine her practice. She was sharing her desire to provide more powerful writing instruction for her students. We had another colleague who was able to accomplish phenomenal feats with her young writers. When Ellen asked this teacher to share what she did to teach and reach her students, she gave Ellen a blank look and said, "I have no idea what it is that I do!" Now the first response was to think that she wanted to keep these secrets to herself. But as Ellen and I became acquainted with coaching processes, we realized that many teachers possess skills and talents that come so naturally to them that they really don't have an awareness of what they do that is different.

As we work with both coaches and teachers, we often prompt them to examine powerful practices they employ through their natural talent and ability. We encourage them to become very conscious of the process they use. It will help them apply this process to areas of weakness in their own practice, as well as offer help to others not naturally gifted in this particular domain.

Coaching! Different Paths for Different People

As you navigate your path for professional growth after 10 or more years of teaching, we want to remind you of the coaching options available to you. You may prefer to have a live experience in which your coach is present with you as you examine an aspect of your practice. We know as coaching catches on (hopefully through your efforts to participate and promote it), you will find your coach is being stretched beyond the ability to always be available to you. Finding ways to work with other colleagues can augment the menu of options. Your coach can be the key in helping choose people who can best meet your needs, as well as facilitate the scheduling of these peer-coaching activities.

Don't forget the power of technology. Capturing a lesson on videotape for a coaching conference can serve an entire team of colleagues. Your coach may have to model the courage it takes to do this by allowing you to tape her teaching in an area in which you wish to grow. Hopefully, you will see that allowing your teaching to go public in front of your coach and peers is a powerful way to build your own confidence in the process of professional growth. It will also help ease your colleagues into taking that brave step. Remember, it takes a good measure of courage to do the right thing for yourself and your students. We believe you will look back on that step with pride and appreciation for what you accomplished. This brave action you take is the hallmark of the teacher who is smokin'! We bet your action will fan the flames in others.

Reflection

If you are at this critical juncture, what will you do to maintain a good path for continuous improvement and professional growth?

What choice will you make—yield to the temptation of the status quo? Develop a highly refined filter to discern what should never change and what should be altered? Foster a culture of coaching with beginning teachers as well as veteran colleagues?

Fading or Going Out in a Blaze of Glory

"Everyone who remembers his own educational experience remembers teachers, not methods and techniques. The teacher is the kingpin of the educational situation."
—Sidney Hook

Though neither of us has yet reached this pinnacle, we have enjoyed the company of many colleagues at this final stage in their careers. One such person comes to mind for both of us. Carol York, former supervisor of language arts/writing, served as our district team leader for language arts for a number of years. She provided us with a magnificent model of mentoring, coaching, and support as we served on the district reading team. As her retirement date grew near, we found ourselves becoming more and more frantic as we sought to capture all Carol could provide to guide us on our paths. We knew her availability to us would soon become limited. We soaked up all we could in those last days of Carol's service and kept in constant contact with her, even after her retirement. We still find ourselves running to her for advice, mentoring, and coaching. We are so grateful for her willingness to still embrace our need for her guidance. How sad it would be for us and all those we support if we had allowed Carol to merely fade away. She possesses a vast amount of knowledge and experience that illuminates our path. How less effective our work would be if we failed to recognize the value in tapping this rich source of wisdom.

As Carol grew closer and closer to her retirement date, we noted that her view of our work became highly reflective and framed in a "big picture" sort of way. Conversations we shared truly supported us in gaining real perspective on where we had traversed together and the next steps that needed to be taken. It took a shared understanding from Carol and both of us to reap the benefits of what she had to offer. We recognize that she has perspective at her juncture not yet available to us. Carol showed a willingness to recognize an ongoing responsibility to her peers—one which maximized her personal and professional contributions. Our relationship of professional respect and personal connection has evolved over time. How fortunate for us to have worked with Carol! It is our mission to help you realize the powerful force you can be as you reach this glorious point in your career path.

So, what do you do as you reach this point in your professional path? We bet by now you knew the answer before we posed the question! It is the support of a coach who can help you identify the strengths you possess and avenues available to share your wealth with your peers. We hope you will seriously consider doing this so the generations of students to come will reap the benefit of your talents, wisdom, and efforts. What follows are some suggestions to get you started on your way to a blazing finish to your career.

Tapping Your Innate Gifts

Remember the story about the teacher who had no idea she possessed such natural gifts in teaching children to write? Allow your coach to help you assess your talents and identify the gifts you have to bestow. Use your coach to devise a method that can effectively capture and share your parting gifts to your colleagues. Remember, an effective coach spends 90 percent of his or her time looking for strengths (Barkley 2005). Your coach can serve you by helping you learn to do this for yourself. The use of videotapes may be a powerful tool for accomplishing this part of the task. Once you identify your gifts, you are able to begin the work of becoming conscious of what you do in your process of teaching and supporting students through this gift. This consciousness, or metacognitive awareness, of your teaching enables you to answer important questions: What am I doing? Why am I doing it? How can I improve? What are my criteria for success? Such questions apply to examination of your instruction as well as the ways that you help students become aware of their own learning. Here, your coach can be a valuable source of support as together you explore questions and situations that reveal how you accomplish what you do.

Tapping Your Rich Experience

By now you have most likely experienced the gamut of what most teachers will face during their teaching career. What have you learned along the way in working with programs, students, parents, colleagues, administrators, and other factors that helped you stay out of those proverbial ditches? How have you learned to prioritize your energy and effort to make the most of every day spent in your classroom? Over the years, you have likely witnessed the seemingly ever-present pendulum swings in educational research, theory, and practice. How many times have you said to yourself (or to colleagues), "That's what we did in the 1980s (or some other relevant period) with a new label." You now possess the advantage of perspective because you have been part of trends—old, new, and recycled.

Tapping Your Accumulated Wisdom

You have seen numerous trends, fads, and practices come and go. Think about the filters you have built that help you discern what will make a difference in the lives of your children. Think about what you do to determine what should remain constant and what needs to be updated and changed. Think about the importance of growing in this wisdom so your practice evolves and keeps pace with the ever-changing demands that our learners will face as they leave our classrooms and enter the workforce.

Advocate for All

We find that many teachers approaching retirement can serve as a powerful voice for all. Teachers at this place in their career have gained much from their experience that can help us grow together. They can be a guiding force for what needs to happen for both students and teachers.

Coaching! Different Paths for Different People

As we pointed out with our experience with Carol York, it will take action from both parties to extend the advantages of your wisdom to your peers. Who better than your coach to help you in this regard? Coaches forge trusting relationships with teachers in order to develop individual plans that will best support them collectively and individually. Lean in and let your coach guide you as you blaze down the final bend of your journey.

Reflection

How can you ensure that all you have worked so hard to accomplish will have the greatest possible impact?

What can you do to leave a legacy that reaches beyond your finite years of service to influence the lives of generations to come?

Who can help you forge this last bend in your journey in such a way that you do more than ever to support learning?

Slowing Down to Speed Up

Thoughts About Coaching

- Coaching is about taking time to focus on your successes.
- Coaching is about feeling rewarded when your students succeed.
- Coaching is about knowing how to pace yourself—personally and professionally.
- Coaching is recognizing that change in routines can have positive outcomes.

Some Observations About Paying Attention

An Attentive Bellhop: Our Hotel Experience

We recently traveled to a conference in Toronto and were most impressed by the personal touch our bellhop employed as he helped move our luggage to our room. Upon reaching our room, he called us by name and commented on our hometown, Tampa, Florida. He then proceeded to share local elements of the weather and nearby sights. He pointed out the stark contrast of Toronto to what we were used to experiencing in Tampa. We were floored by his ability to personally connect to us in such a meaningful way. We commented to the desk clerk about this unusual touch of customer service. She smiled and said, "Oh, that must be Joe. He always takes an extra moment to read the tags on the luggage so he will know our guests by name and where they live."

We were moved by the power of that extra moment of time taken in such a busy place. We began to think of other places where taking an extra moment to ground oneself in a bit of knowledge can lend so much power to the effectiveness of our actions. We thought of NASCAR drivers who know the value of slowing down to take pit stops at certain points along the way to the finish line. We could share countless examples that exemplify the importance of taking time to assess, plan, and reflect on our actions to ensure that we reach our goal of meeting the needs of our students. Taking precious moments to really know our students and to form meaningful connections with them is invaluable to our efforts as teachers. It is knowing when to slow down in order to reach our intended goals that will help us arrive not only alive but fully satisfied as well.

Pacing Ourselves

> *"It does not matter how slowly you go, so long as you do not stop."*
>
> —*Confucius*

We recently heard the saying "slow down to speed up" (Knaus 2007), and it has become a mantra for us. We realize that in all areas of our work and all aspects of our lives there is great truth in examining our practice, as well as how we live our lives. We want to ensure that we are purposeful in all we do in order to avoid the emptiness of mindless motions. Every now and then, it serves us well to slow down just long enough to take a good look around and see where we are in the grand scheme of things. Just like the NASCAR driver, we need to make pit stops. We need to take time for an occasional "dipstick check" of our practices to determine if we are teaching with purpose or slipping into the mindless motions of routines. Engaging in a coaching experience can provide a barometer to measure our practices. Coaching can help us judge for ourselves if our teaching meets the measure we hold in our minds for ourselves as teachers and for the students we serve.

Today, educators are under more stress than ever before. We are held to higher standards and accountability than were the generations of teachers before us. As accountability continues to press in on all sides, it seems as if we are engaged in an ongoing pursuit of trying to master every single aspect of our job all at the same time. We can easily find ourselves becoming "jack of all trades and the master of none."

Technology offers a whole different set of ironies. Though it has made our jobs easier in some ways, in many other ways it causes us to work longer hours than ever before. The simple act of reading emails seems to consume more and more of our time. We also find ourselves tapping online resources for research and cutting-edge information. Many sites offer online coaching experiences. Despite the advantages and conveniences that technology offers, we feel a word of caution is in order. One of the most troubling aspects of our technology age is the temptation to become even more isolated from our peers. We need to remember the value of teaching in the company of others. No aspect of technology can understand and embrace all the human aspects of teaching and the demands that teaching places on our lives. Keeping a perspective on technology as one tool we can use (along with our work with peers) can add a new dimension to our professional growth. We simply need to ensure a balance in the resources we tap.

Let's get back to the notion of slowing down to speed up. One of the most effective elements of coaching is that it requires us to slow down for a short period of time. It invites us to take a look at one aspect of our work to study, reflect, and refine within a particular topic or domain. Once we identify an area or aspect we want to study, we are ready to engage in a coaching experience. We will need to decide just how our reflection on our practice will occur. Will it involve looking on as a peer? Will we study a video of ourselves teaching? Will we begin this process by inviting a peer to watch and capture data that will show us what we need to know?

Contexts for Coaching

Coaching can take place in many domains. These can range from basic management routines to high levels of content knowledge and sophisticated instructional techniques. Similarities exist in coaching for these different aspects of teaching. However, *when* you choose to focus on one particular domain over another can determine whether your coaching experience is one that reaps great reward or frustration. We often experience frustration when we try to obtain expertise in a domain that is dependent upon the strength of more basic components that are not yet well established. We must remember that in teaching, as in everything else we learn, first things must come first. If we do not pay attention to laying a strong foundation, we will be attempting to float high-level concepts over voids in our practice. These observations remind us of the discussion of the gradual release of responsibility model in Chapter Five (see pp. 103–106). Working together with your coach through the stages of modeling, observing, and implementing provides opportunities to explore fundamentals before attempting a new or revised task on your own.

Some of the first places we suggest you explore are your routines and procedures. We often find that many teachers are unable to advance in their abilities to reach and teach to student needs because of deficits in this domain. It is important to tackle the more mundane routines in order to free up our minds for the ongoing assessment and thinking that must occur during the act of teaching. We must be able to recognize student needs that are revealed during our teaching and respond to those needs "on the run." We cannot successfully accomplish instructional tasks if our attention and energy are focused on basic routines and behavior issues.

Classroom management is a topic at the forefront of our minds whether we are novice teachers or seasoned veterans. Successful classroom management is vital to running an effective classroom. Students need to know what is expected of them in your classroom. If you want smooth transitions throughout the day, think very carefully about the routines you set in place. Make a list of every possible transition and then come up with a routine or procedure to address it. Including students in making decisions helps create a sense of ownership and improve motivation as they adjust to following the routines. Let them help you create the list of routines and procedures. We have often found that leading a discussion with students and giving the rationale helps build the community within the classroom. No matter what direction you take in examining and refining your classroom procedures, we think there are some basic factors that can guide your thinking. The checklist in Appendix 6.1 (pp. 189–190) provides information about planning, instructional practices, and student awareness, as well as several questions for self-reflection.

Once you have identified an area of routines or procedures you want to improve, you will need to develop an action plan that will move you in the most efficient manner to accomplished practice. This is best and most easily accomplished in the company of a trusted peer, who may be your coach or another teacher. Once you have received information on your current practice and determined where you want to go, your next step is to practice the desired behavior or technique many times and in many ways so that it becomes a natural part of your routine. Once it becomes routine, you can move on to domains of your work that require you to operate at higher levels of sophisticated thinking. In all these activities, your coach can be there as a listener, commentator, and supporter.

Reflection

Identify routines you know are effective in supporting your ability to teach. What features of these routines make them effective?

Are there parts of your instructional time when your attention seems to be devoted to student behaviors that interrupt your routine? How do you currently deal with these interruptions? How would you prefer to deal with them?

What procedures can you identify that you might want to improve or refine? What information about the procedures do you think you would initially share with a coach?

Teaching, Coaching, and Learning

"Everything works when the teacher works.
It's as easy as that, and as hard."
                                    —*Marva Collins*

We have to constantly remind ourselves that learning takes time. In so many instances, we expect ourselves to read something new or attend a workshop and immediately put the ideas into practice. When we try, we find that the reality is not as flawless as the movie we had created in our mind when we were planning our approach to this new concept. Sometimes we find that the results are indeed quite flawed. Do you remember a workshop experience that inspired you to do something new and different? The trainer made it all sound so simple and so clear. You felt inspired and just couldn't wait to try it out in your classroom. But when you presented it to your class, the results were nothing like you had imagined in the planning stage. At that point, many of us quit and go back to familiar practices that are more reliable and predictable. However, if a coach were there to support or cheer us on through the darkest hour of our change process, we could find the staying power to stick with it long enough to achieve optimum results. When we push through the pain of change, we become that teacher in the movie of our mind—the teacher who can teach in a multitude of ways to deal with the multitude of learning styles sitting in front of you. Of course, we realize that achieving the turnaround you are seeking may be affected by a range of factors. Maybe the necessary resources are limited, the administration is unsupportive, you are alone in your desire to change, some individuals are cynical about new ideas, or the value of teacher talk is dismissed. However, by working with your coach and other like-minded colleagues, you can contribute to the development of a professional environment that recognizes the value of instructional coaching. To do so takes courage—something that we talked about in Chapter Two.

The main reason for slowing down to speed up is to maintain a keen awareness of why we do what we do. At a recent coaching seminar, the keynote speaker, Joellen Killion, asked the audience, "What is the purpose for instructional coaching?" The crowd almost unanimously answered, "To support teachers in improving their instruction." She then cleverly pointed us down a path that revealed to us that we were stopping short in our vision and understanding of coaching. She redirected our focus to consider the relationships between teaching, coaching, and student learning. How students perform as a result of our instruction provides the information that enables us to determine what we should continue to practice, what we may want to refine and change, as well as what we may decide to abandon or add to our practice. The purpose for instructional coaching is to impact student achievement positively. As Killion put it, in essence, the teacher is the "vehicle, the pass-through" that connects coaching experiences and instructional practice, leading to improved student achievement. The coached teacher is in actuality the means to an end.

Reflection

Think about a situation in which you attempted to use a new strategy with less-than-desirable results. How could you have worked with a coach to make the situation more satisfying and effective?

All types of coaching are built on the premise that the person coached will learn new and improved ways of working, which will provide greater benefit to himself or herself and his or her clientele. Defining the clientele or the end user is a critical step we must take in laying out a path for coaching that will be purposeful and will prove profitable to both the person being coached and the clientele being served. Whether it is the football player who is coached to kick more effectively in order to score more field goals, or the teacher who works to change pedagogy in order to better reach and teach students, it is important to keep a well-defined focus on who it is really about—the end user, or the customer. In the case of the kicker, it is the fans. The kicker and the team he or she serves work collectively to serve up a winning game for their fans. In our case, it is the teacher, coach, and school working collectively to serve up a steady diet of success for the students.

> *"Coaching ultimately transfers to students, who enjoy a heightened passion and skill on the part of their teacher. Coached teachers are fiercely alert to their practice. They reflect on how they achieve learning in their students with other professionals, whose focus and desire is to support them in achieving success."*
> —Steve Barkley

Now we have come to a whole new set of ponderings. Hopefully, the first realization you will make is to discard the notion that coaching is about judging your teaching behaviors as good or bad. This falls short of the goal for coaching and distorts its purpose. Have you ever been frustrated by a player on your favorite team who puts himself or herself before the good of the team? We call them prima donnas or accuse them of "hotdogging." They seem to be upside down in their vision of who is serving whom. They demand a lot of attention and when their performance flounders, they often blame the team, don't they? They seem to miss the point of what they do and for whom they do it. Put simply, they have not yet realized that it is *not* about them! To truly serve their purpose, they must embrace the fact that they serve a team that in turn serves the fans. It is really about the fans. Where would the team be without the fans?

As teachers, we must avoid such pitfalls and remain clear on who is serving whom in the classroom. Coaches serve teachers as a means for serving students. In the combined efforts of the coach and the teacher, we must remain focused on whom we both ultimately serve—the students. We cannot expect our students to arrive at school in a certain way that will make our work easier. We must embrace them for who and where they are and begin devising our work in a manner that will serve them. Learning is not about the coach. Learning is not about the teacher. Learning is about the students and what we are able to do to help them reach their optimal levels of achievement.

Keeping our intended purpose and target in focus requires us to turn our attention to finding out about our students. Your coach should be standing beside you as you look at your students both on paper and in action. Data—both qualitative and quantitative—needs to be collected and analyzed. The current emphasis on high-stakes testing ensures that teachers have access to lots of quantitative data. However, data derived from what happens every day in the classroom offers more realistic and practical sources that you can use to shape your instruction. For example, you and your coach can note how students respond to the teacher and each other during the lesson. Do the responses confirm that the students understand the concept being taught? Do they listen to each other in discussion or when answering the teacher's questions? Do they use language consistent with the lesson topic or concepts? In such a setting, you or your coach can track the accuracy of student responses within selected categories (e.g., correct answers, approximations in answers, off-base answers, listening to each other, and so on). When the lesson is over, you can reflect and see which responses demonstrated evidence of understanding and which students went down a different path. If you are looking for quantitative data in this type of activity, have your coach record tallies for the number of correct responses versus the number that were off track. Observing students in a variety of settings and activities at different times provides additional sources of information about their achievement. These observations help you answer the question, "What do I know about my students as learners?" Suggestions for collecting evidence through observations are included in Appendix 6.2 (p. 191). Reflecting on your teaching, thinking about the ways that you guided student thinking in one direction or another, and talking with your coach all enable you to determine what does and does not work for your students. It is through this kind of self-analysis that we become more effective teachers.

We teach to foster our students' growth in a myriad of ways. Some of these ways are measured in numbers obtained through testing, while others are measured through more subtle forms of evaluation. Would any of us like to think that the time and energy we devote to our students are solely for the purpose of capturing a higher number on a test? A test score is merely *one* indicator that tells us if we have been successful in our endeavor to advance students beyond the place that we found them. We need far more evidence than a single score on a test to know we accomplished all we desire for our students. We hope to see that as a result of our efforts, they have evolved as thinkers, decision makers, and citizens. We want to be assured that we have helped them grow as individuals. We want to know that we helped our students in building a sense of purpose for their lives that reaches beyond themselves and helps them find their places in the larger world of society. And isn't it possible that in *that* process, we as teachers tap the same process for ourselves? *That* is the purpose of coaching. It is the act of committing oneself to a larger force that can indeed create change—one school, one classroom, one teacher, and one student at a time. As Wheatley has observed, "All change, even very large and powerful change, begins when a few people start talking with one another about something they care about" (2002).

The ultimate message we want to convey to you is that doing anything with precision and professionalism requires us to slow down and clearly define our visions and goals so that each and every action we take moves us to a higher level of refinement. Ellin Keene reminded us and our colleagues about the value of slowing down to speed up when she observed, "We need to slow ourselves down to give ourselves time to really do *deep* thinking" (October 2007).

Reflection

What telltale signs indicate that you need to "slow down to speed up"?

Do you feel that you are losing your sense of purpose because you are getting lost in the ongoing tasks and daily demands of teaching? Share these observations with your coach or a colleague.

What type of coaching experience would help you refocus your lens and recapture the purpose of why you do what you do?

Navigating Your Own Coaching Path

Thoughts About Coaching

- Opportunities for coaching partnerships exist in every school.
- Collaborative efforts with colleagues sustain professional curiosity and growth.
- Coaching can sometimes be self-directed.
- Coaching recognizes that teaching is the activity most clearly responsible for student learning.

Some Observations About Getting Help

On Automated Telephone Systems and Coaching: Cheryl's Story

I recently arrived home to find my dad talking on my phone. It was a strange-sounding conversation that caused me to pause and listen. He was speaking in one-word sentences at a volume and with an intonation that was not normal. As I continued to listen, it became clear to me that he was trying to report that his own home phone was out of order. I couldn't help but get tickled as I heard him repeatedly bark out the answers to each prompt, sometimes repeating each answer several times. As the call proceeded, he began to sound more and more agitated. His responses became louder, slower, and more pronounced. This usually incredibly patient man was beginning to get red in the face and shake with anger. It just became funnier and funnier to me as I heard him repeat one word utterances of No! Yes! Yes! then his phone number, again and again. This went on for a good five minutes. The longer it went on, the more I laughed.

I laughed, I am sure, because I was experiencing how I look and sound when dealing with automated voice menus. After many attempts to share his information, he finally reached his breaking point and yelled into the phone, "Kiss my foot and call me!" He then proceeded to yell my phone number and abruptly hang up.

I am lucky my dad is a good sport. He accepted my laughter at his discomfort and in fact joined me. We had a hysterically good time laughing together, followed by a litany of complaints about the lack of a human touch in situations where we find ourselves in need. As teachers, we often find ourselves in a place where we need that human touch—a touch from someone who is "in our skin" and really "gets" the human aspects we experience as teachers. We know that many teachers will find themselves in a setting where no coach is available to them. So what do you do? How do you find a way to examine your practice effectively without a person to support you in this important process? Even if you have a designated coach now, it is quite possible that the coach will not always be available when you have something to discuss or share. Although we are most privileged to work in a district that is forward-thinking in developing and supporting the role of coaches, we still have schools with no allocation for this position. Furthermore, many of our schools *with* full-time coaches are finding that the demand for coaching is exceeding what one individual coach can provide.

There are several avenues we can explore to help you find the support you need as you work to improve what you do each day in the service of your children. In this chapter we describe peer coaching, along with activities in which teachers work with coaches and/or colleagues to examine, reflect upon, and change their current practices. We hope this description helps tie together the many ideas about coaching that we have shared in previous chapters. We also describe situations in which teachers engage in what we are calling "self-directed coaching." Sometimes circumstances are such that teachers have no alternative but to take the initiative to explore their own practice without the assistance of colleagues. So buckle up as we move down the last few miles of our journey together.

Reflection

In what settings have you exchanged ideas about teaching with friends and colleagues?

What features of these settings made your conversations worthwhile?

What resources can you draw on to foster professional conversations in the absence of a coaching program?

Reflecting on our own practice is not an easy task. What resources or events have helped you become more sensitive to what you do in the classroom?

Peer Coaching

"Teachers learn best by studying, doing, and reflecting; by collaborating with other teachers; by looking closely at students and their work; and by sharing what they see. This kind of learning cannot occur in college classrooms divorced from practice or in school classrooms divorced from knowledge about how to interpret practice."

—Linda Darling-Hammond

This is the next mile marker on our road to developing ourselves as professionals. The concept of coaching can be cultivated without a designated instructional coach based in the school. Although we are advocates for school-based coaches, we recognize that these positions will not be present in every school. In fact, we go so far as to say that successful coaching does not depend solely on a school having a designated coach. Peer coaching provides an alternative. The key to peer coaching is that there are people in the school who share a vision and are dedicated to the pursuit of improvement in their profession. These people view coaching as an opportunity to learn new instructional strategies and to seek innovative ways to approach teaching. They do not see coaching as a way of fixing what is wrong, but instead view collaboration with peers as a way of taking what is already effective to much higher levels for themselves and their students. When taking this view, the courage to look at what may need to be changed becomes part of a natural process of professional growth.

Peer coaching can take many forms that we will describe in this chapter—co-teaching, inclusion classrooms, cross-age tutoring, model classrooms, professional learning communities, book studies, and action research. We look at peer coaching as a partnership between two (and sometimes more) professionals who are willing to reveal strengths and weaknesses to each other. Let's take a peek at what we're talking about in the next scenario.

Teachers Working Together: Mary's Story

I started teaching at a new school three years into my new career as a classroom teacher. I was beginning to get a firm understanding of procedures and routines as a relatively new teacher, but lacked a depth of knowledge in the art and science of teaching. Actually, the art of teaching came somewhat naturally to me, but I was very conscious of the fact that I still had a great deal to learn about the science of teaching. Back in those days there were no designated coaches, but peer coaching existed informally.

Fortunately, I happened to share a wall with a very experienced teacher who had stretched out her arms to me on many occasions when I first arrived at this school. We worked out a plan to bring our two classes together every Friday to try out new teaching techniques in the presence of each other. Sometimes she would teach the class and I would circulate and tend to student groups or individuals. Other times I would teach the lesson and she would circulate. At the end of the day, we would talk about the successes and the challenges, plan a new approach for the following week, and repeat the process over and over until we had both learned from each other's unique gifts and talents. It was also very comforting when we knew we could laugh at our mistakes at the end of the day.

We gathered a tremendous amount of data from our students that we might not have, had we operated in isolation. One exceptionally easy and helpful way we captured data was to take turns circulating around the room while one of us was teaching the lesson. As we circulated, we jotted our observations on sticky notes. When we noticed that certain students were grasping a concept, we noted that. Conversely, when we noticed that some or all students were not able to apply what was being taught, we also made notes. At the end of the lesson we would examine the notes and talk about what we had observed. This exchange allowed us to plan more effectively for the next lesson. It was especially helpful to place the sticky notes in a composition book that we kept over time so that we could examine patterns and trends in teaching and learning.

In retrospect, our teaching could not have been as responsive and targeted to student needs if we did not make the commitment to meet on a regular basis to talk openly with each other. We kept the level of respect for each other's teaching as our highest priority. When we kept the focus on the children and not on each other, *we operated at a much more energized level because we were both in this to figure out the puzzle of teaching. We knew that we could be each other's solution to it! Our collaboration made our teaching more focused and precise. We understood the value of explicit instruction that guided student learning. We learned from each other how to improve our lessons by taking into account what we had observed as we circulated among the students. We tried new things that turned out to be successful, and we also learned what to abandon along the way. The dialogue was very collaborative, and we never crossed the boundaries of judgment or evaluation with one another. That was my first taste of peer coaching. I guess that positive experience is what sparked my interest in making it a career path. At the time, I had no idea that the things we were doing were considered "best practices" or even had special names like "gradual release of responsibility, collaboration, or coaching." We were just following our teaching instincts!*

> *"We come to understand things better through talk…I may have actually passed geometry had our teacher let us talk."*
>
> —*Ellin Keene*

Co-Teaching

We suspect our district is not unique in its need to make the greatest use of limited space. As a result, we have an increasing number of co-teach classrooms in our schools—classrooms in which two teachers share responsibilities in order to accommodate requirements for student-teacher ratios. This organizational structure provides a built-in everyday opportunity for coaching. The real danger here is falling into the trap of taking your situation for granted so that you no longer realize the opportunity it provides.

If you are lucky enough to be in a co-teach situation, we entreat you to embrace this time spent in the company of a peer to enter into coaching activities. Start simply and watch it grow. Teaching day after day in the company of a peer will provide the perfect scenario for parading your teaching in a manner that will propel you to improved practice. It may be tempting to shortcut past the necessary time to talk, but remember, it is the scrutiny of our experience that holds the power for positive change. It is through this sharing of thought that we will gain a different perspective that can help us grow. Luckily, there will be countless opportunities to naturally engage in talk that is student focused and provides the context for examining your practice with your peer. What an enviable position you hold with this provision of daily encounters with a peer—a peer who knows your students as well as you do. It is this common platform of shared knowledge that can catapult you to higher levels of professional growth.

Inclusion Classrooms

A variety of models exist for providing the specialized support many of our students need. When this support is provided in the context of the general education classroom through a push-in model of support, we have a built-in opportunity for coaching similar to that of a co-teach classroom. The difference is that the opportunity most likely occurs for only part of the day. This model also involves teachers with different backgrounds coming together to serve the same students. We believe this is a situation that is also quite enviable. How fortunate it is for our students when *two* professionals with *two* different areas of expertise converge on the instruction provided to them. What a tremendous opportunity to grow in your knowledge of reaching and teaching *all* students.

We have worked with many ESE (Exceptional Student Education) teachers and not only can we learn from them but they are just as eager to learn from us. When we face the challenge of teaching students with unique and often perplexing problems, it only makes sense to lean in and learn from one another. As general education teachers, we have had numerous opportunities to learn new teaching strategies in all of the content areas of the curriculum. However, many of us "Gen-Ed people" have not had the extensive behavioral strategy training and background that our ESE colleagues have had. On the other hand, many of our ESE partners, as rich in knowledge as they are in the understanding of human behavior, have not had the same number of professional development opportunities that many general education teachers have had in developing curriculum knowledge. It only stands to reason that we have a lot to offer each other if we are willing to take the time and effort to listen and learn from one another.

Remembering to keep our eyes trained on our students will always keep us focused on a path of professional growth. We owe it to ourselves to run—not walk—to embrace such opportunities. Our students are depending on us to do just that!

Cross-Age Tutoring

Cross-age tutoring offers another vehicle that can provide opportunities for peer coaching. In this scenario, teachers from different grade levels work together to provide tutorial experiences for their children. The older students are assigned to the younger students to work on a specific skill or merely provide guided practice. This approach offers great benefit to both sets of students. For the younger student, the impact is obvious. However, for the older child, the process of internalizing knowledge in order to impart it to the younger student has a profound effect on his or her learning as well. As reported in the Cross-Age Tutoring and Online Tutoring Handbook (http://ozpk.tripod.com/crossage), not only do students who are tutored benefit but the students who do the tutoring also benefit, often more so than those who are being tutored. We have both found that cross-age tutoring produced serendipitous effects on our teaching. Though our primary purpose was to provide support and reinforcement for our students as they worked with peers from other grade levels, we also received support and reinforcement from our peer teacher. We have discovered that a peer can offer keen insights and fresh perspectives in regard to what we do as teachers, as well as what our students' behaviors are begging of us. Having a peer at our side improves and sharpens our skills as student watchers. Knowing how to look for clues and cues and how to interpret what they are telling us is key to moving our practice forward to meet student needs. As suggested earlier in this chapter, it is the observation of students and the collection of student data that provide the material for rich conversations between teachers—conversations that will goad their thinking in new directions. As teachers work to monitor and support the cross-age tutoring activities, they informally assess what is happening with students—both the tutor and the tutee. As they share their observations with one another, they begin to reflect on what students are doing well and where additional instruction and support are needed. It is this process of reflection based on what students reveal that provides the vehicle for professional growth. We emphasize that professional reflection is best accomplished when we keep a student-focused approach and make decisions about what to change in our instruction based on what our students are doing, as opposed to opinions and judgments rendered on the teacher's behaviors.

Model Classrooms

If there is one thing we have learned in this journey of teaching, it is that every teacher must have something valuable to offer his or her students and peers, or he or she simply would not be able to remain in this profession. In some schools, teachers enter their classroom with the intention of operating in "private practice" mode. Eaker observed, "The traditional school often functions as a collection of independent contractors united by a common parking lot" (Eaker, as cited in Schmoker 2006, 23). Operating in isolation limits the teacher and students as well as colleagues who surround this classroom. Furthermore, "…isolation masks the starkly different results achieved by different teachers. Without any point of comparison, the isolated teacher never has to confront the fact that (1) the teacher next door may be three times as effective as I am, or (2) much of my teaching is inferior (though parents and principals seem to like me as much—*or maybe more than*—that teacher next door)" (Schmoker 2006, 24).

Our experience supports the observation that "teaching is too tough to go it alone" (Routman 2000, xlii). With this quote, we celebrate the unique strengths in each of us that can be used to learn from each other. Observing in each other's classrooms is a useful way to learn from each other. Some teachers are masters at reaching their students through conversations within the classroom. Others have cultivated incredible learning environments and each wall of the classroom has clear evidence of the learning that occurs each day. There are also teachers who have routines and procedures down to such a precise science that the students know exactly what to do at any given moment of the day. None of us proclaims to have everything we need to be the perfect model teacher, but each of us possesses a gift that can be shared with others to widen our repertoire of skills. Model classrooms are everywhere; it just depends on what it is you choose to focus on.

Professional Learning Communities

> *"The professional learning community model flows from the assumption that the core mission of formal education is not simply to ensure that students are taught but to ensure that they learn. This simple shift—from a focus on teaching to a focus on learning—has profound implications for schools."*
> —*Richard DuFour*

When you choose to be part of a professional learning community, you are making a conscious effort to reduce teacher isolation by working with a team of professionals at your school. Your goal is to increase commitment to the mission and goals of the school, create shared responsibility for the total development of all students, create powerful learning opportunities that promote good teaching and classroom practice, and enhance understanding of student standards and teacher roles.

If done well, professional learning communities can produce higher job satisfaction and improved morale because they give a voice to teachers who might otherwise remain silent and alone in their classrooms. To develop a community of learners in your school, pull interested and willing people together. Start talking about constructing a shared vision. Just as with other types of coaching, it is imperative to develop trust and relationships that will nurture a program of collaborative learning for all. This will allow you to have honest and frank discussions about where the learning of your collective professional development needs to go next.

Strong leadership is a critical factor in the success of professional learning communities. Hopefully, you have an administration that is motivated and enthusiastic about supporting such a strong component of professional development at your site. If such vision is not currently in place, this could be your opportunity to shine.

Book Studies

You have an enormous amount of control over your own learning and the development of your teaching. One of the most common ways that teachers can share their experiences with each other is through mutual study of a professional book. Much like Oprah Winfrey's Book Club, we can approach book studies in a manner similar to the one she has used to ignite thousands of people to become excited about books and reading. For example, our dear friend, colleague, and respected resident guru of reading, Cristie Mosblech, recently came to us with a book titled *Comprehension Through Conversation* (Nichols 2006). With book clenched tightly in her hand, she passionately spoke of its profound effect on her and its potential value to us. She proceeded to share some of its content with us and enticed us with short snippets that she read aloud. She gave specific examples of how it aligned with our vision and where we wanted to move with our own learning. Before you knew it, we were ordering it, reading it, referencing it with each other, and ultimately sharing it publicly with as many people as possible. It gave us all a common language that worked to strengthen our professional relationships with one another and provided us with a unified voice for moving forward together in a specific direction. We are just as excited to read Nichols' new book, *Talking About Text: Guiding Students to Increase Comprehension Through Purposeful Talk* (2008).

Action Research

> *"Curiosity is one of the permanent characteristics of a vigorous mind."*
> —Samuel Johnson

Ever have a burning question that just won't go away? Our burning questions usually point to some unknown obstacle that prevents our students from making the progress we hope to see. If you have such an issue constantly circling your mind—congratulations! This curiosity is your first step on a journey to new knowledge and professional growth. One of the most exciting ways to discover what you seek can be found through action research—the focused exploration of a specific teaching strategy or topic within the classroom. However, we find that not many teachers jump at this opportunity when we mention the words *action research*. We think we understand why. We have very strong images that flood our minds when we hear the word *research*. We think lab coats, sterile environments, and rigidly controlled variables. With this picture in mind, we often think there is no place to practice research in our classrooms. We invite you to rethink that notion. It is in the company of others that we can discover that we are not alone in having confounding questions that beg to be answered. Action research can provide just the vehicle you need to start unraveling those mysteries that occur within the classroom. As you identify a nagging question for which you have no answer, you can begin your own investigative process—either alone or in the company of peers. You may find that all of the aforementioned tools can help you find answers to the questions you hold concerning your students. You do not have to don a lab coat and reconstruct your classroom, but merely make a decision to move into investigative action. It is through a process of looking and learning that you will gain insight into those burning questions.

Through the contributions of some of our colleagues, we can share with you a firsthand experience with action research. Katy Cortelyou, one of the Reading First coordinators, was assigned to work with Dianna Steffen, a reading coach, and a group of teachers in order to conduct action research about a burning question. In the story that follows, we have captured the perspectives of all involved in this research. The story includes Katy's work with Dianna, the site-based coach, as well as reflections from two teachers who represent the team involved with this professional development activity.

Action Research: Katy Cortelyou Shares Her Experience

During a spring visit to Bryan Elementary, Dianna and I were pouring over year-end assessment data. In our search for trends across grade levels and classrooms, a puzzling question surfaced. We noticed strengths in second-grade students' Nonsense Word Fluency (NWF) scores but considerable weaknesses in their Oral Reading Fluency (ORF) scores. It was from this discrepancy that our action research question was born! We asked how complex phonics skills specifically impact oral reading fluency. Armed with a question, we quickly sprang into action by holding a year-end meeting to propose the project to the second-grade team. Although it was with great exuberance that Dianna and I spoke about the action research, we felt a great sense of uncertainty on the part of the teachers. After the meeting, Dianna and I chuckled to ourselves, thinking we would be lucky to have one willing participant in the new school year! So it came as a great surprise when we learned just days later that all seven teachers were interested in participating in the action research initiative.

Having proposed this idea at the end of the 2005–2006 school year, it wasn't until the fall of the 2006–2007 year that our plans really began to take shape. In September, we met to discuss the criteria for selecting our focus students, the lesson routines we would implement to target our research question, and the tools we would use to monitor student progress relative to our research question. It was also during this first meeting that we addressed logistical concerns such as how often we would meet to share progress and problem solve concerns. Although we agreed to meet monthly, Dianna and I had to be flexible in order to accommodate the teachers' busy schedules. We actually only met three more times as a group but provided ongoing classroom support through data collection, modeled lessons, and follow-up coaching.

While Dianna and I were certainly energized by the coaching opportunities and professional dialogue that resulted from this project, we still hadn't answered our initial question related to phonics and oral reading fluency. However, as year-end data was collected, we made some enlightening discoveries. In looking at both students' accuracy percentages on grade-level text and their words read per minute, we found marked improvements in both areas. It was with great anticipation that we called a final meeting of the year. Dianna and I had data spreadsheets ready to share, but before we could even do so, the teachers were leading the conversation. We listened with such pride as they shared the successes of their focus students and formulated curriculum plans for beginning the routines at the very start of the 2007–2008 school year. At the end of the meeting, Dianna and I just looked at each other and said, "What a difference a year makes!" given that we went from thinking we would have no participants at all to witnessing teachers who had clearly moved to a powerful place of self-reflection and autonomous learning.

Thinking back, Dianna and I maintain that the action research was a success because we invited teachers to explore a question that was relevant and meaningful. Additionally, we approached this project with the goal of "building the plane as we flew it" in an effort to be sensitive and responsive to teachers' professional development needs.

As noted in Katy's description of the action research project, all seven second-grade teachers in Bryan Elementary were involved in the project. Here are reflections from two of the teachers, as well as Dianna Steffen, the reading coach.

Reflections on the Action Research Project

"I found the action research project grew my professional knowledge and provided new tools to support me in meeting my students' needs. I feel as though the phonics survey is a useful assessment tool for beginning second graders. It gives me a jumping-off point. The mat lessons from the Beck book are very useful in teaching students word study skills such as word patterns. We continue to use the mats for guided reading mini lessons." (Maggie Rodriguez, Second-Grade Teacher, Bryan Elementary School, Plant City, FL)

"An action research project was formed to address the need for fluency, and we were coached monthly by both Katy and Dianna (and more often as needed by Dianna). We then used specific lessons to build fluency depending on each student's phonics needs. I added a piece with my students in which I conferenced with each student after their DIBELS® test scores were returned, and we discussed each area and what was needed to make the next timed target. Many students left with a sticker on their hand that I printed with the slogan, 'Speeding Your Reading.' For all my students, it was the first time a teacher had discussed their reading skills in this manner and had given goals for testing. Because of this intervention, I believe my students benefited, and data supports it by showing gains for those students targeted in the action research.

As far as the coaching experience, I had never allowed myself to be closely coached before. Although I am a 'seasoned' teacher, at first I was intensely uncomfortable with the idea of being watched and monitored. However, both Katy and Dianna allowed the experience to be relaxed and student oriented, and as a result, I became much more comfortable with being coached.

I am following up the action research experience this year with a similar format for my students by using DIBELS® to sort their needs and targeting specific skills for intensive intervention. Had I not had the experience with the action research at my school, I would not understand how to use the DIBELS® scores to target specific skills for intervention purposes. I believe I benefited from the experience, but the gain was truly for my students." (Laura Lyons, Second-Grade Teacher, Bryan Elementary School, Plant City, FL)

"I have never been so honored to be working as a coach and being given the opportunity to grow alongside these remarkable teachers. Because of the information we learned from the action research project, we are trying something new this year. We have implemented Beck's lessons in all first grade as II (Initial Instruction) instead of III (Immediate Intensive Intervention) to help build a solid foundation. I thank you for allowing me the opportunity to share, and I am so proud of what we all have learned and how we all have grown. This has done more than answer our question about second graders' reading fluency—it has caused coaching relationships to blossom." (Dianna Steffen, Reading Coach, Bryan Elementary, Plant City, FL)

 ## Reflection

Which of the peer coaching activities described have you engaged in? What did you learn from these experiences? What would you change when doing these activities again?

Which activities that you haven't used would you like to try? What arrangements will you have to make to carry out the activities?

Self-Directed Coaching

> "I have come to feel that the only learning which significantly influences behavior is self-discovered, self-appropriated learning."
> —Carl Rogers

We must take individual responsibility for our professional needs, especially in situations in which support through coaching or professional learning communities is unavailable. There are countless ways we can pursue professional development on our own. The remainder of this chapter will explore some of the methods for coaching ourselves to achieve better practice. You may have other options that you wish to explore. The ideas we share are by no means the only vehicles available to you. We merely hope to spark your thoughts and inspire you to take a step forward—a step that leads you down a path of positive change and rewarding results.

Videotaping

As we mentioned in Chapter Four, if you really want to take a true look at your teaching, videotape a lesson or two and watch yourself as you interact with your students. Using videotapes as professional learning tools is growing in popularity. Becky Hinson videotaped herself teaching as part of the portfolio she created while seeking certification from the National Board for Professional Teaching Standards. She had this observation: "Videotaping myself teaching was one of the most worthwhile experiences I had. You see yourself doing things that you don't know that you do" (Hinson, as cited in Richardson 2007a, 1).

In the absence of a coach, videotaping your lessons can be one of the most powerful reflective tools you can use. But we must share a few cautions. Please remember you are often your own worst critic. At the outset, ensure that you have a clear purpose for why you are videotaping yourself. When you watch yourself on the video, try to be as objective as you possibly can. Treat yourself as a professional and focus on points that are truly meaningful to improving your teaching. Concentrate on the instructional characteristics of the session, particularly noticing the strengths of your approach. Try making a list of the effective interactions you had with your students that led them to the places you intended. It's okay to make a list of things that you feel could be improved upon, but don't make that your sole focus. If you only focus on needs, you will never want to see yourself on videotape again and that would eliminate one of the most powerful tools you have at your disposal. Stigler, a proponent of using videotapes for professional development, is nonetheless skeptical about the value of a teacher watching his or her own practice on tape. "Looking at yourself can be very threatening… If you videotape the way you teach, you're not going to learn a new idea. Even after you start looking at yourself, you can still have blind spots if you don't have colleagues sitting there with you while you're viewing the videotape and critiquing your teaching" (Stigler, as cited in Richardson 2007a, 2).

For this reason, we hope that you can find the courage to go one step further and share your videotape with a trusted colleague and together analyze and discuss what is shown. Stigler maintains that the analysis and discussion that follows the watching of a videotape is where real learning occurs. As you share your observations, do not be surprised to find that you have sparked ongoing dialogue and coaching interactions!

Do not limit the use of this tool to personal reflection. We have many coaches who use video as a way to enhance the work they do with teachers. They often videotape themselves or the teacher. Having a lesson on tape provides opportunities for teachers to watch at their convenience, either alone or in the company of another professional. So take that first step that will lead you to becoming that star teacher you envision yourself to be. You might want to take another look at suggestions for observing and analyzing videotapes presented in Appendix 4.3 (pp. 183–184).

Audiotaping

Also discussed in Chapter Four, we have heard from many teachers that an audiotape is a useful way to comfortably self-analyze verbal interactions in the classroom. When you don't have access to feedback or coaching from a colleague, listening to and analyzing an audiotape can provide very useful information. It allows you to zoom in on a particular point you are trying to convey to your students without the visual distractions that sometimes haunt a video clip. For example, in reading instruction, we have found audiotaping to be quite useful when teachers analyze their strategy instruction with students (see Appendix 4.4 on pp. 185–186 for suggestions about analyzing audiotapes). We have also used a form on which teachers can record examples of their strategy talk and student responses (see Appendix 7.1 on p. 192). The information recorded on the form enables teachers to analyze their word choices as they guide students to monitor their own reading. By analyzing student responses, teachers can determine whether they are being too supportive or not supportive enough in their approach to teaching self-monitoring techniques. Most of all, the analysis narrows the focus for refinement, which is essential in any attempt to refine your practice.

Online Resources

Online resources for professional development are almost limitless in number. We often use some of these resources to learn about what the experts are saying, to guide our thinking, and to prod our forward movement. We do not align ourselves with any one single expert or organization. It has always been our stance to glean pieces from many experts that most closely match our philosophy and vision. We often rely on professional books to inform us, but occasionally we find that online resources from a professional organization provide a more global perspective. We acknowledge that these online resources are targeting a wide audience and may not address your specific needs. The important concept to embrace here is that the more we read, research, and explore, the more empowered we become to make informed decisions. We have listed some of our favorite websites in Appendix 7.2 (pp. 193–195). We hope you find something in these resources to empower you in your journey to reach higher in your pursuit of excellence.

Becoming a Teacher Leader

"All teachers can lead! Most teachers want to lead. And schools badly need their ideas, invention, energy, and leadership."
—*Roland Barth*

We hope that through a variety of coaching experiences, you have been inspired to reach out and grow—to become a teacher leader. Remember, you are in charge of your learning. Whether or not you have a coach at your disposal, you have many options. So take a deep breath, summon your courage, and take off down the path of professional growth—a path *you* design. We bet that your commitment to grow will lead others to follow in your steps. There is a teacher leader inside just waiting to burst out! Start moving yourself to the destination you seek—a destination where you will reap the benefits and satisfaction of a job not just *well* done, but *best* done!

Reflection

What coaching opportunities are available to you?

Which of these opportunities have you used and found beneficial? What may you have overlooked in other opportunities?

What part does coaching play in your professional growth plan?

Do you view yourself as a teacher leader? Why or why not?

As a teacher leader, I will commit to…

Taking the High Road

8

Thoughts About Coaching

- Coaching leads to enhanced professional awareness.
- Coaching lends credibility to strengths.
- Coaching fosters realistic perspectives about change.
- Coaching builds self-awareness and self-confidence.

Some Observations About Potential Pitfalls

Before this book concludes, it is important to speak to issues that without some forewarning could land your coaching efforts squarely in a ditch. It has been our experience that the higher the road you choose to travel, the deeper the ditches you will find beside it. The more passion you fuel for the sacred work before you, the more risks you will be willing to take. The more risks you take, the greater danger you have of landing in one of those ditches.

Throughout this book our intent has been to provoke thinking and honest evaluation of your actions so that you can keep your eyes focused on the road to professional growth. Avoiding the ditches will require some honest disclosure on your part. The careful planning in the company of others can help to avoid the dangers of the ditches. *Remember the value of slowing down to speed up!*

> *"All education is continuous dialogue—questions and answers that pursue every problem on the horizon."*
> —William O. Douglas

As you grow professionally and your wisdom expands, you will likely discover many opportunities to share a ditch experience with peers to help them avoid the consequences you encountered when you inadvertently took a wrong turn. By the same token, you will want to learn from the experiences of others to glean similar advantages for both you and your students. Coaching comes to us in many forms—some coaching experiences are informal, while others are part of a formal institutional structure. The power of any collegial coaching experience lies in the sharing of thoughts and ideas through talk. Often it is through the simple sharing of our stories that collegial dialogue will begin to pave the way to powerful coaching experiences.

Keep a Balanced Focus

No matter who is involved in the examination of practice, you must ensure that a healthy balance is struck. If we focus only on the areas of sure-footed practice or on areas of concern, the lack of balance will limit the positive impact of the coaching experience. We want to be able to see and celebrate accomplishments, as well as identify targets for growth. We need to learn to do this for ourselves as we engage in self-reflection, as well as when we work with colleagues.

Focusing only on what is troublesome or difficult can lead to discouragement and the potential to abandon coaching activities altogether. The most effective coaches we know spend more time recognizing and pointing out practice that is effective and hitting the desired target for students. These coaches use this context of strong practice to prompt reflection about places that invite change or refinement.

On the flip side, only focusing on strengths will prolong the task of addressing areas of deficit or concern. If you are truly seeking to refine and improve your practice, this delay can be frustrating. If you walk away with no ideas for improvement, you may not wish to engage in future coaching experiences. This is quite understandable given the time constraints teachers face. Not one of us feels we have a moment to waste on anything that has not shown itself to have real value.

Each year as we train new coaches, we observe issues that create ditches for our trainees. Some will become so focused on their shortcomings that they are tempted to quit each day. Other coach candidates begin to engage in what we call a "love fest," in which their feedback consists only of compliments that can be bestowed upon one another.

So how do you achieve and maintain a balance? The most efficient way to accomplish this desired balance is by keeping your coaching experiences focused on the students. Remember, it is all about the *students*. By looking to the students for evidence of what is working, we can discern which components of our teaching are truly effective and which components merit a closer look.

Reflection

Think about the topics that you have discussed with a colleague or a coach. To what extent do these conversations center on successes? On difficulties? On problem situations?

Remain True to the Purpose of Coaching

In remembering that the purpose of coaching is to impact student achievement, we are compelled to point out some ditches that must be avoided in order to stay true to this purpose. We have stood in the shoes of both classroom teachers and coaches. We understand the dynamics of the relationships each builds with his or her colleagues. Allow us to share some of our experiences as coaches that have forced us to stop, reflect, and try to understand why we often landed in ditches when working to support teachers. At the risk of sounding negative, we want to help you understand how coaching and collaborative relationships can become dysfunctional. By becoming aware of the ditches, we believe that it is easier to act in ways that enable us to avoid them.

Can reasons for coaching be wrong or misguided? Yes! When we encounter teachers who don't see the value of coaching and collaborating to increase student achievement, we are asked to do things in the classroom that have absolutely nothing to do with the desired outcome—improving student achievement. We have experienced occasions when a teacher wanted to catch up on paperwork or make a phone call, so the coach was invited into their classroom to "model" a lesson. Once the coach arrived and began to teach the lesson, the teacher very quietly slipped out the door and returned much later to thank the coach for teaching such an effective lesson to the class. Other times, the teacher stayed in the classroom but spent the time getting caught up on paperwork and not participating in the activities the coach provided for the students. This is *not* coaching by any stretch of the imagination! Instead, these actions are a cleverly disguised extra planning period for the teacher. As we have noted throughout this book, coaching is a cooperative effort in which teachers and coaches use their combined knowledge to build more effective learning experiences for students.

What other ditches do we need to avoid? Teachers often ask coaches to do a tremendous number of assessments on students—tasks that take enormous amounts of time. This is time spent away from classrooms, teachers, and instruction. Admittedly, sometimes assessing students is a much easier place for a coach to operate. You get to spend time one-on-one with students, people see you as a hero for doing tasks they would rather not do, plus it gives you a reprieve from resistant teachers who do not want you in their classrooms. What we have learned, and hope that you also recognize, is that most people who enter into coaching have a true passion for teaching and working with their fellow educators. When this situation fails to happen on a regular basis, many coaches become discouraged and move on to other roles in education, thus leaving a vacuum in which there is little to no potential for change to occur—change that could lead to improved instruction for students. There is nothing more deflating to us than not being able to interact with fellow teachers and seek ways to refine practice in order to bring the lifelong love of learning to more students. On days when your energy runs low, you may be tempted to ask your coach or a collaborative partner to do things to make *your* life better but not necessarily better for the students. Yes, it's easier to have someone else assess your students, but you are the one who teaches them. Much of what is gained from assessments lies in the nuances you observe as you assess. A coach may try to convey all the nuances, but much will get lost in translation. In such cases, the benefits of assessing for student strength and need are compromised.

On many occasions, teachers have asked us to pull groups of students and teach them. This request seems to be made in recognition of the expertise we bring to the situation. Trust us when we tell you that the offer to work with students is very tempting to a coach. We can even justify our work as having real benefit to the students we instruct. However, it does nothing to build collaborative relationships that will lead teachers to more refined practice that can positively impact student achievement over time. We must constantly measure the benefit of short-term and immediate outcomes against those that can make enduring differences over the long haul. You may encounter similar situations as you attempt to engage in collegial coaching with your peers. You may find that when you pull your students together with another class with the intent of collaborating, it will be tempting to use that time to chat rather than see it as an opportunity to take steps toward enduring improvement in your current practice. You can stay true to your purpose if you continuously ask yourself, "How will my current actions have a positive impact on the achievement of my students?"

Know When to Back Up and Change Directions

A Mother's Example: Cheryl's Story

My mom provides the perfect example of "knowing when to back up and change directions"—a principle we must embrace if we are truly committed to making the very best happen for students. A large part of Mom's time is spent doing cross-stitch projects. She embraces two purposes for engaging in this activity. One purpose is to claim victory over the arthritis that threatens to cripple her hands. Her second purpose is to bless the homes and special events of people she knows and loves. She works endless hours on these projects. I check on her progress periodically, and almost without exception she spends most of her time telling me what she had to rip out and do over. You see, she often has a different vision for the final product than the company who packaged the craft kit. She will determine that a different color would work better for the effect she desires. She is undaunted by the fact that hours of her time are about to be undone. She never focuses her attention in that way, but keeps her sights pointed forward to reach the destination she has created in her mind. I marvel at her willingness to go backward in her progress in order to obtain a higher goal—a product of perfection and the satisfaction of knowing she did all she possibly could to make each quilt or wall hanging the very best it could be.

"Who dares to teach must never cease to learn."
—John Cotton Dana

The story of my mom's experience provides a wonderful background for discussing the biggest and most difficult hurdle we seem to face in our quest for reaching the pinnacle of our practice: our inability or unwillingness to back up and find a better way of doing things that haunts our efforts to improve. For most of us, we have learned to teach in a certain manner that has become comfortable and predictable. If we are not careful, our behaviors can become "embedded in concrete," such that we can't advance because we can't see alternatives—we are stuck! In such a circumstance, we can easily begin to see teaching as merely a number of activities we must check off our list each day. Although we may embrace the need for new strategies born of recent research, we fear the effort that will be required to fit one more item into an already overstuffed day. This is a real concern that invites us to enter into the most difficult part of backing up to change directions. It is the fear of letting go that often hinders our forward progress. We resist the notion that we have possibly been engaged in practices that fall short of our goal for our students. We also fear that if we remove that one faulty thread, the fabric of our daily routines will completely unravel. It is this fear, added to the difficulty in admitting our practice is not perfect, that often causes us to cling to the old and familiar. We wonder if sometimes we don't actually believe that if we alter our ritualized practice, we may lose some magic force contained within the familiar ways. We are reminded of the superstitions so many athletes practice. For instance, we are drawn to the pitcher who must go through certain rituals before throwing each pitch or the golfer before swinging the club.

As coaches, we have seen again and again the seemingly impenetrable words of resistance, the familiar chimes—"I've been doing it this way for 10 years and it always worked for *me*!" "I don't see anyone else doing things differently." "You don't understand these kids—I have to work with them in this way." The mirror we wish to hold for teachers is one that reflects these words in a manner that can reveal just where we get off track in our underlying motives for what we do. If we are truly honest with ourselves, we will begin to see the flawed thinking in these words. Through thoughtful examination, we can begin to see that we have indeed lost the focus that can make all the difference— keeping the students front and center for the purpose of why we do what we do. Students are the reason we began our journey in the world of teaching. It is important that we continue to take action based on the true purpose we sought when we first answered this sacred call to teaching. We must become comfortable with new ways of thinking about and approaching our craft. We must recognize that we are not perfect but are willing to constantly undergo self-examination and reflection with others in order to continue our quest for improvements. Simply

stated, our vision of perfection is arriving at the place where we can rest assured that we are doing all we possibly can to keep a student-focused approach—an approach that invites reflection for improvement each and every day.

Learn to Discern: Am I Moving Instruction or Merely Managing Behavior?

Teachers face many challenges as they work with their coaches to refine their instruction techniques. Giving up practices that have been in place for years is one of the biggest. We have found that examining these practices closely for their underlying reasons and benefits often helps to identify those which are not promoting student growth to the fullest.

For example, one of the most common practices on which we work with teachers is to help them change their understanding of how to implement independent activities for their students. Dominating many classrooms are the unending supplies of worksheets that students are required to complete each day. In these situations, we invite teachers to examine this practice from a number of angles and perspectives. We see teachers spending countless hours preparing this work, spending more time providing the directions to students than students take to complete the work, and then spending additional time grading each paper. When we question teachers about this particular routine of practice, we begin to divulge thinking that has actually betrayed the teacher into believing these worksheets are serving a purpose that is not actually ever realized.

Let's walk through some self-examination that will provide a guiding light for this practice. What is the purpose of the worksheet? For most teachers, when they brave the task of truly questioning the practice, they realize that this is an issue of classroom management, not sound instructional practice. They recognize that they are merely using the worksheets to keep certain students occupied while the teacher focuses on a small group of students who need extra attention. When teachers honestly contemplate what the worksheets provide to them, in terms of information gained about their students, they are often surprised with the conclusions they reach. The typical worksheet is actually an assessment that reveals what students have within their control. Teachers often discover that this type of independent activity only reveals what students already know and are able to do. The students who could do this work obviously did not need the practice, and those who could not do the work found no support that furthered their ability to complete the activity successfully. Consequently, such a task is unlikely to provide any new information about student performance. Teachers arrive at a second set of alarming data when they track the time they must take to give directions for worksheets. Once they are able to discern the difference between giving directions and explicit instruction, they see that they have been losing precious instructional time. When teachers reach this point in their reflections, they are dismayed that they have spent so much time standing absolutely still in the progress toward greater student achievement. You might be interested in taking another look at the topics related to self-analysis of classroom routines in Appendix 6.1 (pp. 189–190).

Who Benefits From Change?

We must remain steadfast in our efforts to filter what we plan to do each day in order to meet the ever-changing needs of our students. As more is learned that shines new light on our current practices, and as we seek better ways to prepare our students for a rapidly evolving workplace, we must have some way to measure the effect that any new practice may have on student achievement. Remembering to keep this perspective will help us stay out of those dangerous ditches. Results of any decision we make—either to remain steadfast in current practice or adapt our teaching to move differently—must always come down to assessing the advantage we see for our students. We want to remain genuine in our analysis and continually strive to find the powerful and doable actions that we can take. The key is ensuring that what we ask of ourselves is not more than we can possibly deliver and manage, and that each action we take does in fact move our students in the direction we want them to go.

The perfect action is one that is a win-win for both the students and the teacher. This is where ongoing coaching can provide the greatest support for teachers. It is in the company of a trusted colleague that a teacher will be able to analyze accurately what impact a practice is having on student achievement, as well as the demands that it makes on the teacher.

> *"The true aim of everyone who aspires to be a teacher should be not to impart his own opinions, but to kindle minds."*
>
> —Frederick William Robertson

What Source of Information Is Driving My Decision to Change?

When we decide to take a step in a new or different direction, we must be acutely aware of what is prompting this action. We need to be data driven to ensure that we are purpose driven. Personal considerations may come into play as we decide to move in a new direction. Perhaps you want to teach another grade level, teach another subject, move to another school or district, or work toward attaining a position in administration, consulting, or coaching. Sometimes teachers choose to move to educational enterprises outside of school districts; for example, working as editors, consultants, or sales professionals with publishing companies. Whatever the source of your motivation to make a change, you will be gathering information that enables you to reach a decision that is best for you. More than likely, the information you collect will include quantitative factors (e.g., working conditions, experience and qualification requirements, salary, benefits), as well as qualitative factors (e.g., lifestyle change, friendships, interpersonal relationships). Likely, you will talk with colleagues, friends, and family about your desire to pursue new career directions and opportunities.

Similarly, when you decide to modify your teaching practices, you will want to employ a variety of data sources to determine the directions you can take to provide more effective instruction for your students. Student data should reach far beyond standardized test scores or other indicators we are often required to capture. We should attend to this information but also pull in many other data sources that will help us paint a more accurate and complete picture of the impact we wish to have on our students. We hope you will find your way to analyzing soft data (qualitative analysis) in addition to hard data (quantitative information). Soft data often provides the information that is the greatest catalyst for moving hard data in the positive direction we desire. (See Appendix 6.2, on p. 191, for suggestions about collecting data through observations of students in various settings and activities.)

We have found that teachers who are most successful and satisfied in their practice are those who are able to promote learning in ways that enable their students to monitor and analyze their progress for themselves. We see this actualized in the way that their students often begin to develop their own feedback mechanisms that provide a fast track for the teacher in determining what steps need to be taken next. It is in the course of becoming tuned in to the nuances of student signals that our greatest progress as teachers is hailed. It is attending to what our students reveal to us through their verbal and nonverbal behaviors that often provide the most effective window into the power of our practice.

> "When we understand...we concentrate intensively, we are fervent, we lose ourselves in the experience of thought, we work intensively, the world disappears and we work hard to learn more, we choose to challenge ourselves."
>
> —Ellin Keene

An effective instructional setting where teacher and students are engaged

We must be proactive in planning what we do each day with a purposeful end in mind, but that is merely the beginning. As we engage in the actual practice of teaching, our eyes and ears must be fixed on what is happening with our students as the lesson unfolds. As this becomes our practice, we will learn to teach in a responsive manner guided by our students. It is through this ongoing, reflective process that we will know we are meeting their needs. We will indeed know that we have reached a point in our paths that will promote the very best for ourselves, our peers, and most of all, the students we serve.

Final Reflection

What thoughts about coaching are most prominent in your mind now that you have come to the end of this book?

How have coaching experiences enhanced your level of self-confidence as a teacher?

What expectations do you have for future coaching experiences?

Think about this statement, "Teaching is not a profession, it is a passion." In what ways are you passionate about teaching? How do you think your passion for teaching is communicated to your students? To your colleagues? To your friends? To students' parents or caregivers? How does your passion for teaching help sustain you when things become difficult?

Look at the quotations in Appendix 8.1 (pp. 196–199) to identify those you'd like to discuss with your colleagues. Try out the suggested activities with colleagues in professional development or faculty meetings. In your professional journal, record your favorite quotes about teaching and learning, and reflect on what these messages mean for you.

Appendices

Appendix 2.1: Coaching Options for High-Level Teaching and Reflecting

Teacher:_____ Coach:_____ Date:_____

Coaching provides many opportunities for teachers to examine and reflect upon their practice. Here are some topics for you to consider as you think about how you can work with a coach.

Big Picture: Observing the learning environment

( ) Organization/management _____

_____

( ) Resources/ideas _____

_____

( ) Assessment data _____

_____

Before the Lesson: Planning

( ) Instructional focus_____

_____

( ) Format _____

_____

( ) Lesson flow/timing _____

_____

( ) Whole group: students included _____

_____

( ) Small group: students included_____

_____

( ) Materials _____

_____

( ) Student-to-student talk _____

_____

( ) Teacher-to-student talk _____

_____

During the Lesson: Observing student responses

( ) Clear Instructional focus _____

_____

Appendix 2.1: Coaching Options for High-Level Teaching and Reflecting *(cont.)*

( ) Background knowledge about topic _____

_____

( ) Lesson flow/timing _____

_____

( ) Transitions (e.g., to another idea, to independent work) _____

_____

( ) Student-to-student talk _____

_____

( ) Teacher-to-student talk _____

_____

( ) Student time on task_____

_____

( ) Student follow-up _____

_____

( ) Gender differences _____

_____

( ) Other considerations_____

_____

After the Lesson: Reflecting on what happened during the lesson

We noticed_____

_____

_____

We decided _____

_____

_____

Identifying the next step(s)

_____

_____

_____

Hillsborough County
PUBLIC SCHOOLS
Excellence in Education

Appendix 4.1: Coaching Plan

Having a plan helps both the teacher and coach focus on important topics and make the best use of the time they have available to work together. Think about how you might adapt this sample plan to suit your own purposes.

Teacher: _____ Coach: _____ Date: _____

Content Area: _____

Assessment Data:	Instructional Focus:
Coaching Focus:	Time Frame:
Goal:	Lesson Structure: __large group ___small group __individual
Results/Follow-Up:	

Lesson Plan

Start Time:	
Lesson Core Time:	
End Time:	

Hillsborough County
PUBLIC SCHOOLS
Excellence in Education

Appendix 4.2: Coach Visit Checklist

Preparing for a coach's visit to your classroom takes into account several factors that will ensure that the visit is a success for all concerned—you, your students, and the coach.

	Classroom procedures/routines are posted for visitors to access.
	Seating arrangements have been established.
	There is a designated place for the coach to sit or stand.
	The students understand the role of the coach in the classroom.
	Work areas for teaching are clearly defined.
	Schedules for teaching are posted.
	Materials for the lesson are displayed and accessible.
	Materials will be provided by the coach.
	Materials will be provided by the teacher.
	Whole-group or small-group instruction format parameters have been established.
	Time has been set aside for a teacher/coach conference.
	Student practice opportunity has been planned.

Notes and Reminders:

_____
_____
_____
_____

Hillsborough County
PUBLIC SCHOOLS
Excellence in Education

Appendix 4.3: Video Observation and Analysis Checklist

Introduction

Videotaping of lessons is one of the most reliable means of documenting and observing what actually happens in the classroom. This observation guide provides suggestions for self-evaluation but may also be used to focus discussions with colleagues.

As you watch your video, concentrate on just one or two elements in the lesson. The same video may be viewed several times with a different purpose for each viewing. For example:

- First viewing: Consider how different the lesson was from the perceptions you had of it while you were teaching.
- Second viewing: Identify a particular aspect of teaching you want to examine closely.
- Third viewing: Analyze specific aspects of your behaviors that affect student behaviors, either positively or negatively.
- Fourth viewing: Watch the entire video to identify what you want to capture in future recordings.

Teacher: _____ Class: _____

Date Recorded: _____ Date Analyzed: _____

Classroom Interactions:

- Teacher questions
- Student responses
- Seeking clarification from student responses
- Teacher talk—clarity of vocabulary, supportive language, tapping student background knowledge
- Steps in modeling a strategy
- Wait time
- Dealing with distractions
- Students listening and responding to each other
- Teacher-student interaction
- Student-student interaction
- Students' individual work
- Group work—pairs, small groups
- Giving directions
- Closure to the lesson

Awareness of Students:

- Students you usually look at while talking
- Reasons for focusing on these students
- Engaging disengaged students
- Eye contact with students
- Lesson pacing—signals that help students follow the direction of the lesson
- Position in the room during whole-group instruction
- Movements in the room during group work
- Use and distribution of materials

Appendix 4.3: Video Observation and Analysis Checklist *(cont.)*

- Classroom procedures and routines
- Voice projection and control
- Body language

Classroom Environment: What do you see in the classroom?

- Teacher's desk and things on it
- Furnishings
- Seating arrangements that facilitate interaction
- Display areas and what is displayed
- Learning resources
- Traffic patterns
- Items that personalize the classroom
- Other

Example of Note-Taking Format

Beginning of Lesson:
During Lesson:
End of Lesson:

Appendix 4.4: Audiotape Analysis Checklist

Introduction

Audiotaping of lessons is an effective way of learning about talk in the classroom—the teacher's talk as well as that of the students. This observation guide provides suggestions for self-evaluation but may also be used to focus discussions with colleagues.

As you listen to the audio recording, concentrate on just one or two elements in the lesson. The same recording may be listened to several times with a different purpose for each session. For example:

- First time: Consider how different the lesson was from the perceptions you had of it while you were teaching.
- Second time: Identify a particular aspect of teaching you want to examine closely.
- Third time: Analyze specific aspects of your talk and how students respond.
- Fourth time: Listen to the entire recording to identify what you want to capture in future recordings.

Teacher: _____ Class: _____

Date Recorded: _____ Date Analyzed: _____

Classroom Interactions:

- Teacher questions—types, frequency
- Student responses to teacher's questions
- Student questions—types, frequency
- Seeking clarification from student responses
- Teacher talk—clarity of vocabulary, supportive language, tapping student background knowledge
- Who is doing most of the talking—teacher? students?
- Steps in modeling a strategy
- Wait time
- Dealing with distractions
- Students listening and responding to each other
- Teacher-student interaction
- Student-student interaction
- Group work—pairs, small groups
- Giving directions
- Closure to the lesson
- Voice projection and control
- Lesson pacing—signals that help students follow the direction of the lesson
- Noise level—busy, engaged

Appendix 4.4: Audiotape Analysis Checklist *(cont.)*

Example of Note-Taking Format

Beginning of Lesson:
During Lesson:
End of Lesson:

Appendix 5.1: Gradual Release of Responsibility Lesson Plan

Name: _____ Date: _____

Reading Strategy: _____ Grade Level: _____

Text: _____ Author: _____

Gradual Release			
"I Do"			
"We Do"			
"You Do"			
5 minutes			
10–25 minutes			
Can be done another day or after "we do"			
Mini-Lesson Focus: Great readers use…			
Teacher Talk:			
Chart/Model: When we read that part about… (Pages of the lesson are marked with sticky notes to share my thinking on 2–3 solid examples.)			
Cooperative Learning Link:			
Independent Practice:			
Group Share:			
Teacher Reflection:			

Hillsborough County
PUBLIC SCHOOLS
Excellence in Education

Appendix 5.2: Coaching Collaboration Checklist

Teacher:_____Coach:_____ Date:_____

When working with colleagues in your classroom, following some basic guidelines will ensure that the collaboration is positive and effective.

_____Decide on a date and time to work together (and STICK TO IT).

When: _____

_____Look at formal and informal student data together BEFORE planning lessons.

What: _____

_____Plan lessons together for equal ownership of responsibility.

How:_____

_____Decide who will teach and who will observe student responses.

Who: _____

_____Both colleagues should take turns teaching and observing lessons.

Who: _____

_____Have classroom rules set for students for BOTH colleagues to reinforce consistently.

How:_____

_____Negotiate in advance the physical format of the students' seating arrangements.

How:_____

Other things to think about to help with accountability:

___ Collecting/assessing student work

___ Reporting to parents and administrators

___ Gathering materials/making copies

___ Bringing two classes together at one time

___ Both colleagues agreeing to stay in the room supporting each other

Hillsborough County
PUBLIC SCHOOLS
Excellence in Education

Appendix 6.1: Classroom Routines Self-Analysis Checklist

Teacher: _____ Date: _____

Effective routines are vital to making a classroom successful—a place where students are engaged, and learning is purposeful. Here are some basics for you to think about as you reflect on your classroom routines. A rating system is provided to help you rate the consistency of your routines. Additional questions are included to guide your reflections.

Routines	Always	Usually	Sometimes	Rarely	Never
Planning:					
• Teaching plans, notes, and materials well organized					
• Lesson topics posted by day/week					
• Assignment topics/tasks posted					
• Objectives clearly stated; related to standards					
• Criteria for success defined					
• Alternatives defined in event that the lesson doesn't go as planned					
• Resources appropriate for topic and students' learning needs/interests					
• Procedures for transitioning among lesson activities defined					
• Activities differentiated to meet students' needs/interests					
• Independent activities extend student learning					
• Group practices varied according to students' needs					
• Observations about student learning used to determine next steps					
• Reflections recorded about areas needing more attention					
Instructional Practices:					
• State lesson objective or focus explicitly (e.g., We are learning to…)					
• State criteria for learning success (e.g., We know we will have learned when we can…)					
• Review lesson focus periodically throughout the lesson					
• Review focus at end of lesson					
• Inform students about plan for following the lesson					
• Use strategies that help students monitor their learning					
• Make connections between new material and students' prior knowledge/experience or other lessons					
• Use pace appropriate to students' needs and the topic					
• Vary wait times as needed					
• Make effort to avoid repeating instructions					
• Make students accountable for thinking					
• Make effort to avoid repeating students' answers/responses					
• Employ gradual release of responsibility model					
• Recognize when students need more instruction or guided practice					
• Recognize when students are capable of more demanding tasks					
• Vary voice, gestures, facial expressions to encourage students to participate, to take risks					
• Use a variety of questions					
• Provide opportunities for students to ask questions					
• Adapt lesson activities or time when interruptions occur					
• Vary lesson routines to avoid monotony and boredom					
• Identify parts of lesson that went well, were too challenging, took more time than planned, were out of sequence, etc.					

Appendix 6.1: Classroom Routines Self-Analysis Checklist *(cont.)*

Routines	Always	Usually	Sometimes	Rarely	Never
Awareness of Students:					
• Make effort to know students as unique individuals and learners					
• Know something about students' lives outside of school					
• Be aware of students' interests					
• Make effort to create friendly, supportive, nonthreatening classroom environment					
• Encourage humor and good will					
• Listen actively to students					
• Foster respectful behavior by modeling it					
• Recognize when students are worried, anxious, happy, relaxed, etc.					
• Wait to get attention from all students before starting to deliver instructions					
• Recognize when students are absolutely clear about what they are supposed to do and why					
• Observe student responses/behavior during whole-group, small-group, and individual activities					
• Energize students when their engagement is sluggish					
• Refocus students when their attention is diverted					
• Create a classroom environment that is pleasant and stimulating—a place where students will want to spend time					
• Involve students in decorating the classroom and keeping it tidy					

Planning and Instruction
- Do you think it is important to inform students at the beginning of each lesson about what you plan to do and the objectives you have set? Why or why not?
- Do you think informing students about plans for the next day or days after helps to motivate them? Why or why not?
- What use do you make of homework assignments? How do students respond to homework assignments? What changes would you like to make in the types and use of homework assignments?
- How much time do you spend preparing independent activities? How does this amount of time compare to the time it takes you to give directions for the activity? For students to complete the activity? For you to correct or discuss the activity with the students?
- What data do you collect about student performance? How do you use this data to guide instruction?

Classroom Environment
- How does the organization of the classroom space and seating arrangements facilitate interaction and learning? Inhibit interaction and learning?
- What changes would you like to make in the organization of the classroom space and seating arrangements?
- What would a first-time visitor be most likely to notice about your classroom?
- How would you describe the noise level in your classroom?
- Who do you think does most of the talking in your classroom? How do you encourage more student talk? How do you use what students say to guide instruction? To expand their thinking?

Appendix 6.2: What Do I Know About My Students as Learners?

Gathering evidence of students' achievement is an ongoing part of teaching and planning for instruction. Collecting evidence from a variety of settings and activities at different times enables you to get to know your students as learners and to discover what they bring to the learning process. This data is useful in discussions with a coach about teaching.

Sources of Evidence About Student Performance
- Observe students as they work independently.
- Observe students working in pairs, in small groups, in whole group.
- Observe students as they come into or leave the classroom.
- Make anecdotal notes.
- Review student journals, learning logs, writing portfolios, reading folders.
- Conduct interviews with students.
- Conference with students about selected projects/assignments.
- Have conversations with students—both casual and formal.
- Analyze samples of student work collected over time.
- Show students how to assess their own learning.
- Have students participate in peer assessment activities.
- Have students contribute criteria for use in selected assessment tools (e.g., rubric for story writing, guidelines for group discussions, steps in solving math problems, sequence for demonstrating a science concept).
- Conduct group discussions in which students can talk about or describe their learning.

Tips for Collecting Data
- Schedule times for systematic observations of individual students.
- Identify students to be observed and determine the focus for the observations.
- Keep a clipboard or sticky notes on hand for continuous note-taking of observations.
- Customize observation tools to fit the subject you teach.
- Describe what the student is able to do or what the responses reveal about his or her understanding (e.g., *He knows that he sometimes confuses* b *and* d. *She understands how to use questions to predict outcomes in fiction and is now ready to use questions to make predictions when reading nonfiction text.*).
- Use reporting forms provided by the school, district, or instructional coach to organize the data collected.

What to Look for During Observations
- Student engagement during the lesson—interest, attention, listening ability, responses to teacher questions, interactions with other students, willingness to expand on responses, ability to use scaffolding guidance, ability to overcome distractions that divert attention
- Student engagement during independent work—use of time, focus on the task, ability to accomplish the task, self-direction in moving to another task
- Student engagement during work with a partner, in a small group, in the whole group—attention to task/topic; turn-taking behavior; willingness to contribute ideas; willingness to listen to other students; ability to exchange ideas/respond to peers; ability to get along with peers
- Student participation in teacher conferences/interviews—sense of ease/confidence, willingness to share personal information, ability to describe learning strategies, ability to identify difficulties—where and why these occur, willingness to seek help
- Student participation in class meetings—contributes useful ideas to the discussion, listens to peers, respects ideas of others that are different from own, uses questions to get information or clarification
- Student journals, learning logs, writing portfolios, reading folders—evidence of growth over time, changes in nature of material recorded, use of content or strategies presented in lessons, awareness of ways to monitor own learning, evidence that student has pride in own work, evidence of expanded interests and use of learning resources

Appendix 7.1: Self-Analysis of Strategy Talk

Teachers use strategy talk as they scaffold instruction. The teacher's language provides various levels of support to enable individual students to perform tasks successfully. The analysis of strategy talk includes examination of both the teacher's talk and student responses. Using video or audio recordings is an efficient way to do this analysis.

Teacher Name_____ Date_____

Student Structure: Individual _____Small Group _____Whole Group_____

Teacher Strategy Talk	Student Responses
Reflections: How did the teacher talk help build deeper understanding for the students throughout the lesson? Highlight teacher talk that really moved instruction forward (as evidenced in the student-response column).	Reflections: Looking back at the responses, how well did the students understand what was being taught? What evidence showed that? Highlight that evidence.

Hillsborough County
PUBLIC SCHOOLS
Excellence in Education

Appendix 7.2: Online Resources

Alliance for Excellent Education
http://www.all4ed.org

A national policy and advocacy organization that works to make every child a high-school graduate—to prepare them for college, work, and to be contributing members of society. The alliance publishes policy and research reports.

Association for Supervision and Curriculum Development (ASCD)
http://www.ascd.org

A membership organization for educators at all levels. Publications include books and journals. *Educational Leadership* provides articles about all aspects of K–12 teaching and learning.

Edutopia (The George Lucas Educational Foundation)
http://www.edutopia.org

Edutopia Online provides a variety of resources related to innovative teaching and learning and exemplary K–12 programs. Resources include articles, case studies, research summaries, expert interviews, and lesson plans.

International Reading Association (IRA)
http://www.reading.org

A membership organization serving educators, kindergarten through adult literacy. Publications include books and journals—The Reading Teacher, Journal of Adolescent & Adult Literacy, and Reading Research Quarterly.

Literacy Coaching Clearinghouse
http://www.literacycoachingonline.org

A joint project of the International Reading Association and the National Council of Teachers of English, this clearinghouse provides resources for literacy coaches at all levels.

National Association for the Education of Young Children (NAEYC)
www.naeyc.org

A membership organization serving educators and child-care workers. Publications include books and journals—*Teaching Young Children*, *Young Children*, *Beyond the Journal* (online publication).

National Council for the Social Studies (NCSS)
http://www.ncss.org

A membership organization serving K–12 social studies teachers. Publications include books and journals—Social Education, Social Studies and the Young Learner, Middle Level Learner.

National Council of Teachers of English (NCTE)
http://www.ncte.org

A membership organization serving educators from kindergarten through college levels. Publications include books, journals, and a weekly e-newsletter—Language Arts, Voices from the Middle, The English Journal, NCTE Inbox (free weekly e-newsletter).

National Council of Teachers of Mathematics (NCTM)
http://www.nctm.org

A membership organization serving K–12 mathematics educators. Publications include books and journals—Teaching Children Mathematics, Mathematics Teaching, Mathematics Teacher, Journal of Research in Mathematics, ON-Math (online journal of school mathematics).

National Middle School Association (NMSA)
http://www.nmsa.org

A membership organization for middle-school educators. Publications include books and journals—Middle School Journal, Middle Ground.

National School Reform Faculty (NSRF)
http://www.harmonyschool.org

A professional development initiative designed to develop collegial relationships, reflective practice, and rethinking leadership in restructuring schools.

National Science Teachers Association (NSTA)
http://www.nsta.org

A membership organization for K–12 educators. Publications include books, journals, and e-newsletters—Science and Children, Science Scope, The Science Teacher, NSTA Express (weekly e-newsletter), Science Class (monthly e-newsletter).

National Staff Development Council (NSDC)

http://www.nsdc.org

A membership organization for K–12 educators. Publications include books, journals, and newsletters—Journal of Staff Development, Tools for Schools, T3—Teachers Teaching Teachers.

National Writing Project (NWP)

http://www.nwp.org

A professional development network for teachers of writing at all grade levels. The site contains many articles about writing instruction, as well as reports on the work of teachers and schools affiliated with the project.

Phi Delta Kappa International (PDK)

http://www.pdkintl.org

A membership organization serving educators at all levels. The Kappan carries articles on topics that include assessment to school leadership and reform.

Teacher Leaders Network (TLN)

http://www.teacherleaders.org

An online community that fosters innovative thinking about teaching and learning through professional conversations, as well as other resources.

Teaching Diverse Learners (TDL)

http://www.alliance.brown.edu/tdl/

Resources designed to enhance the capacity of teachers to work effectively with English language learners are available at this website.

Appendix 8.1: Quotes About Teaching, Coaching, and Learning

We often use quotes to start conversations, to encourage reflection, and to foster an exchange of opinions during our presentations about teaching and coaching. Responses to the quotes can vary, and we use these individual interpretations to facilitate talk among colleagues.

- Sometimes all in the group agree on the message in the quote but offer different interpretations of what it means for them personally.
- Sometimes individuals share stories that illustrate the quote.
- Some individuals disagree or are uncertain about the message and provide stories that illustrate their perspectives.

Throughout the chapters in *Instructional Coaches and Teachers: Sharing the Road to Success*, we have placed quotes throughout the text. We thought it would be useful to have these quotes listed in one place, so here they are—organized in the order in which they appear in each chapter. We hope the quotes stimulate your thinking and conversations with colleagues.

Chapter One: Starting Down the Yellow Brick Road

"One of the beauties of teaching is that there is no limit to one's growth as a teacher, just as there is no knowing beforehand how much your students can learn."—Herbert Kohl (p. 28)

"The disposition for teaching is two percent inborn and ninety-eight percent reinvented every day of one's career."—Susan Ohanian (p. 33)

Chapter Two: Taking the Road Less Traveled

"Unless one has taught…it is hard to imagine the extent of the demands made on a teacher's attention."—Charles E. Silberman (p. 43)

"Teachers should unmask themselves, admit into consciousness the idea that one does not need to know everything there is to know and one does not have to pretend to know everything there is to know."—Esther P. Rothman (p. 48)

Chapter Three: Recognizing Detours and Dead Ends

"Other people can't make you see with their eyes. At best they can only encourage you to use your own."—Aldous Leonard Huxley (p. 55)

"I'm not a teacher; only a fellow traveler of whom you asked the way. I pointed ahead—ahead of myself as well as you."—George Bernard Shaw (p. 59)

Chapter Four: Sharing the Driving

"The more deeply you understand other people, the more you appreciate them, the more reverent you will feel toward them. To touch the soul of another human being is to walk on sacred ground."—Stephen Covey (p. 78)

"Things do not change; we change."—Henry David Thoreau (p. 82)

"Genuine learning always involves dialogue and encounter." —Clark E. Moustakas (p. 88)

Chapter Five: Finding Rewards in Twists and Turns

"Even the best professional development may fail to create meaningful and lasting changes in teaching and learning—unless teachers engage in ongoing professional dialogue to develop a reflective school community."—Regie Routman, 2002 (p. 102)

"Society's greatest opportunity lies in tapping the human inclination towards collaboration."—Derek Bok (p. 104)

"Nobody starts out as a completely effective and creative teacher…The desire to teach and the ability to teach well are not the same thing. With the rarest of exceptions, one has to learn how to become a good teacher."—Herbert Kohl (p. 108)

"Occasionally…what you have to do is go back to the beginning and see everything in a new way."—Peter Straub (p. 117)

"Everyone who remembers his own educational experience remembers teachers, not methods and techniques. The teacher is the kingpin of the educational situation."—Sidney Hook (p. 126)

Chapter Six: Slowing Down to Speed Up

"It does not matter how slowly you go, so long as you do not stop."—Confucius (p. 132)

"Everything works when the teacher works. It's as easy as that, and as hard."—Marva Collins (p. 136)

"Coaching ultimately transfers to students, who enjoy a heightened passion and skill on the part of their teacher. Coached teachers are fiercely alert to their practice. They reflect on how they achieve learning in their students with other professionals, whose focus and desire is to support them in achieving success."
—Steve Barkley (p. 138)

Chapter Seven: Navigating Your Own Coaching Path

"Teachers learn best by studying, doing, and reflecting; by collaborating with other teachers; by looking closely at students and their work; and by sharing what they see. This kind of learning cannot occur in college classrooms divorced from practice or in school classrooms divorced from knowledge about how to interpret practice."—Linda Darling-Hammond, 2005 (p. 145)

"We come to understand things better through talk…I may have actually passed geometry had my teacher let us talk."
—Ellin Keene, 2007 conference presentation (p. 148)

"The professional learning community model flows from the assumption that the core mission of formal education is not simply to ensure that students are taught but to ensure that they learn. This simple shift—from a focus on teaching to a focus on learning—has profound implications for schools."—Richard DuFour (p. 152)

"Curiosity is one of the permanent characteristics of a vigorous mind."—Samuel Johnson (p. 154)

"I have come to feel that the only learning which significantly influences behavior is self-discovered, self-appropriated learning."—Carl Rogers (p. 159)

"All teachers can lead! Most teachers want to lead. And schools badly need their ideas, invention, energy, and leadership." —Roland Barth (p. 162)

Chapter Eight: Taking the High Road

"All education is continuous dialogue—questions and answers that pursue every problem on the horizon."—William O. Douglas (p. 165)

"Who dares to teach must never cease to learn."—John Cotton Dana (p. 170)

"The true aim of everyone who aspires to be a teacher should be not to impart his own opinions, but to kindle minds."—Frederick William Robertson (p. 174)

"When we understand...we concentrate intensively, we are fervent, we lose ourselves in the experience of thought, we work intensively, the world disappears and we work hard to learn more, we choose to challenge ourselves."—Ellin Keene, 2007 conference presentation (p. 175)

References Cited

Albritton, G. 2001. *K–2 Reading coaches initiative formative evaluation report*. Tampa, FL: School District of Hillsborough County.

Alda, A. 2006. Quotable quotes. *Reader's Digest* (November): 85.

Barkley, S. G. 2005. *Quality teaching in a culture of coaching*. Lanham, MD: Rowman and Littlefield Education.

Barth, R. S. 2001. Teacher leader. *Phi Delta Kappan* 82 (6): 443–49.

Bok, D. 2005. Cited in McAndrew, D., *Literacy leadership: Six strategies for peoplework*, 91. Newark, DE: International Reading Association.

Casey, K. 2006. *Literacy coaching: The essentials*. Portsmouth, NH: Heinemann.

Collins, J. 2001. *Good to great: Why some companies make the leap…and others don't*. New York: Collins.

Collins, M. 1997. Cited in *Quotations on education*, comp. Rosalie Maggio, 46. Paramus, NJ: Prentice Hall.

Covey, S. 1990. *The 7 habits of highly effective people: Powerful lessons in personal change*. New York: Simon & Schuster.

Darling-Hammond, L. 1997. *The right to learn: A blueprint for creating schools that work*. New York: Jossey-Bass.

———. 2007. Teacher learning that supports student learning: What teachers need to know. *Edutopia Online*. Accessed at www.glef.org

Dana, J. C. 1997. Cited in *Quotations on education*, comp. Rosalie Maggio, 28. Paramus, NJ: Prentice Hall.

Douglas, W. O. 1997. Cited in *Quotations on education*, comp. Rosalie Maggio, 65. Paramus, NJ: Prentice Hall.

DuFour, R. 2005. What is a professional learning community? In *On common ground: The power of professional learning communities*, ed. Richard Dufour, Robert Eaker, and Rebecca DuFour, 31–43. Bloomington, IN: National Education Services.

Duke, N. K., and P. D. Pearson. 2004. Effective practices for developing reading comprehension. In *What research has to say about reading instruction*, ed. A. Farstrup and J. Samuels, 205–42. Newark, DE: International Reading Association.

Emm, L. 2007. Chat wrap-up: Teacher-directed professional development. *Education Week* 7 (February): 30.

Fullan, M. 2002. The change leader. *Educational Leadership* 59 (8): 16–21.

Goldsmith, M. 2007. *What got you here won't get you there: How successful people become even more successful.* New York, NY: Hyperion.

Haberman, M. 2005. *Star teachers: The ideology and best practice of effective teachers of diverse children and youth in poverty.* Houston, TX: The Haberman Educational Foundation.

Harvey, S., and A. Goudvis. 2005. *The comprehension toolkit: Language and lessons for active literacy.* Portsmouth, NH: Heinemann.

Hook, S. 1997. Cited in *Quotations on education*, comp. Rosalie Maggio, 38. Paramus, NJ: Prentice Hall.

Huxley, A. L. 1997. Cited in *Quotations on education*, comp. Rosalie Maggio, 31. Paramus, NJ: Prentice Hall.

Isaacs, W. 1999. *Dialogue and the art of thinking together.* New York: Doubleday.

Johnson, S. 1997. Cited in *Quotations on education*, comp. Rosalie Maggio, 152. Paramus, NJ: Prentice Hall.

Joyce, B., and B. Showers. 1988. *Student achievement through staff development: Fundamentals of school renewal.* 2nd ed. White Plains, NY: Longman Publishers.

———. 2002. *Student achievement through staff development.* 3rd ed. Alexandria, VA: Association for Supervision & Curriculum Development.

Keene, E. October 31, 2007. The dimensions of understanding. Conference presentation for District Level Reading Team, K–3 Reading Coaches, and Elementary Reading Resource Teachers. Hillsborough County School District, Tampa, FL.

Killion, J., and C. Harrison. 2005. 9 roles of the school-based coach. *T3 Teachers Teaching Teachers* 1 (1): 1–5.

———. 2005b. Data coach. *T3 Teachers Teaching Teachers* 1 (2): 1–2.

———. 2005c. Mentor. *T3 Teachers Teaching Teachers* 1 (3): 1–3.

———. 2005/2006. School leader. *T3 Teachers Teaching Teachers* 1 (4): 1–3.

————. 2006a. Curriculum specialist. *T3 Teachers Teaching Teachers* 1 (5): 1–2.

————. 2006d. Classroom supporter. *T3 Teachers Teaching Teachers* 1 (8): 1–3.

————. 2007. Resource provider. *T3 Teachers Teaching Teachers* 2 (7): 1–3.

Knaus, R. 2007. Multi-tasking: Slowing down to speed up. Accessed October 10, 2007 at *My Article Archive*. http://www.myarticlearchive.com/articles/6/309.htm.

Knight, J. 2007a. Conversations can kick off the coaching. *T3 Teachers Teaching Teachers* 2 (6): 1–4.

————. 2007b. *Instructional coaching: A partnership approach to improving instruction.* Thousand Oaks, CA: Corwin Press.

Kohl, H. (a). 1997. Cited in *Quotations on education*, comp. Rosalie Maggio, 28. Paramus, NJ: Prentice Hall.

Kohl, H. (b). 1997. Cited in *Quotations on education*, comp. Rosalie Maggio, 38. Paramus, NJ: Prentice Hall.

Little, J. W. 1990. The persistence of privacy: Autonomy and initiative in teachers' professional relations. *Teachers' College Record* 91 (4): 509–36.

————. 2007. Teachers' accounts of classroom experience as a resource for professional learning and instructional decision making. *Yearbook of the National Society for the Study of Education* 106 (1): 217–40.

Lortie, D. 1975. *Schoolteacher: A sociological study.* Chicago: University of Chicago Press.

Martin, J. R. 1985. *Reclaiming a conversation: The ideal of the educated woman.* New Haven, CT: Yale University Press.

Morgan, D. 1981. *Laughter: The best medicine 1985.* 12th ed. New York: Berkley Books.

Moustakas, C. E. 1997. Cited in *Quotations on education*, comp. Rosalie Maggio, 65. Paramus, NJ: Prentice Hall.

Mullen, C. 2006a. All in a day's work. *Reader's Digest* (September): 88.

————. 2006b. All in a day's work. *Reader's Digest* (December): 88.

National Center for Education Statistics (NCES). 2007. *Teacher attrition and mobility: Results from the 2004-05 teacher follow-up survey.* http://nces.ed.gov/pubsearch/pubsinfo.asp?pubid=2007307

National Reading First Conference. 2005 (July 25–28). U.S. Department of Education. New Orleans, LA.

Nichols, M. 2006. *Comprehension through conversation: The power of purposeful talk in the reading workshop.* Portsmouth, NH: Heinemann.

———. 2008. *Talking about text: Guiding students to increase comprehension through purposeful talk.* Huntington Beach, CA: Shell Education.

Ohanian, S. 1997. Cited in *Quotations on education,* comp. Rosalie Maggio, 39. Paramus, NJ: Prentice Hall.

Pearson, P. D., and M. C. Gallagher. 1983. The instruction of reading comprehension. *Contemporary Educational Psychology* 8:317–44.

Random House Unabridged Dictionary, copyright ©1997, by Random House, Inc. on infoplease, http://www.infoplease.com.

Richardson, J. 2006. Building confidence is part of the coach's job. *T3 Teachers Teaching Teachers* 1 (8): 4–5.

———. 2007a. Learning through a lens: Classroom videos of teachers and students prove to be a powerful professional learning tool. *Tools for Schools* 10 (4).

Robertson, F. W. 1997. Cited in *Quotations on education,* comp. Rosalie Maggio, 30. Paramus, NJ: Prentice Hall.

Rogers, C. 1997. Cited in *Quotations on education,* comp. Rosalie Maggio, 63. Paramus, NJ: Prentice Hall.

Rothman, E. P. 1997. Cited in *Quotations on education,* comp. Rosalie Maggio, 30. Paramus, NJ: Prentice Hall.

Routman, R. 1996. *Literacy at the crossroads: Crucial talk about reading, writing, and other teaching dilemmas.* Portsmouth, NH: Heinemann.

———. 2000. *Conversations: Strategies for teaching, learning, and evaluating.* Portsmouth, NH: Heinemann.

———. 2002. Teacher talk. *Educational Leadership* 59 (6): 32–35.

Rowley, J. B. 1999. The good mentor. *Educational Leadership* 56 (8): 20–22.

Schmoker, M. 2005. No turning back: The ironclad case for professional learning communities. In *On common ground: The power of professional learning communities,* ed. Richard Dufour, Robert Eaker, and Rebecca DuFour, 133–53. Bloomington, IN: National Educational Service.

———. 2006. *Results now: How we can achieve unprecedented improvements in teaching and learning.* Alexandria, VA: Association for Supervision and Curriculum Development.

Shadowlands (movie). 1993. Directed by Richard Attenborough. Savoy Pictures.

Shaw, G. B. Cited at http://en.thinkexist.com/quotes/withkeyword/teacher/2.html.

Silberman, C. E. 1997. Cited in *Quotations on education*, comp. Rosalie Maggio, 33. Paramus, NJ: Prentice Hall.

Stern, G. 2006. Quotable quotes. *Reader's Digest* (November): 85.

Straub, P. 1997. Cited in *Quotations on education*, comp. Rosalie Maggio, 56. Paramus, NJ: Prentice Hall.

Warren, R. 2002. *The purpose driven life: What on earth am I here for?* Grand Rapids, MI: Zondervan.

Wheatley, M. J. 2002. *Turning to one another: Simple conversations to restore hope to the future.* San Francisco: Berrett-Koehler Publishers, Inc.

Related Reading

Bambino, D. 2002. Critical friends. *Educational Leadership* 59 (6): 25–27.

Berry, B., J. Norton, and A. Byrd. 2007. Lessons from networking. *Educational Leadership* 65 (1): 48–52.

Danielson, C. 2007. The many faces of leadership. *Educational Leadership* 65 (1): 14–19.

Davis, G., and M. Metzger. 2006. Teachers mentoring teachers. *Edge* 1 (3): 3–19.

Donaldson Jr., G. A. 2007. What do teachers bring to leadership? *Educational Leadership* 65 (1): 26–29.

Dozier, T. K. 2007. Turning good teachers into great leaders. *Educational Leadership* 65 (1): 54–49.

DuFour, Richard., R. Eaker, and Rebecca DuFour, eds. 2005. *On common ground: The power of professional learning communities.* Bloomington, IN: National Educational Service.

Honore, C. 2004. *In praise of slow: How a worldwide movement is challenging the cult of speed.* London, England: Orion Books.

Intator, S. M., and R. Kunzman. 2006. Starting with the soul. *Educational Leadership* 63 (6): 38–43.

Keene, E. 2007. *Assessing comprehension thinking strategies.* Huntington Beach, CA: Shell Educational Publishing.

Keene, E., and S. Zimmermann. 2007. *Mosaic of thought: The power of comprehension strategy instruction.* 2nd ed. Portsmouth, NH: Heinemann.

Killion, J., and C. Harrison. 2006b. Instructional specialist. *T3 Teachers Teaching Teachers* 1 (6): 1–2.

———. 2006c. Catalyst for change. *T3 Teachers Teaching Teachers* 1 (7): 1–3.

Remen, R. 2006. *Kitchen table wisdom, 10th anniversary edition.* New York: Riverhead Trade, The Berkeley Publishing Group.

Richardson, J. 2007b. Work smarter, not harder: SMART goals keep key objectives in focus. *Tools for Schools* 11 (2).

Sparks, D. 2007. Changing organizations begins with changing ourselves. *Edge* 3 (1): 318.

Wasserman, S. 2004. *This teaching life: How I taught myself to teach*. New York: Teachers College Press.